THE
SWE

This book shows you   rful
party food, ice cream   and
exotic, tempting tre   ood way!

By the same author
A VEGETARIAN IN THE FAMILY
PASTA DISHES
PIZZAS AND PANCAKES
QUICHES AND FLANS
SIMPLE AND SPEEDY WHOLEFOOD COOK
THE RAW FOOD WAY TO HEALTH
THE WHOLEFOOD LUNCH BOX

THE WHOLEFOOD SWEETS BOOK

by

JANET HUNT

Illustrated by Clive Birch

THORSONS PUBLISHERS LIMITED
Wellingborough, Northamptonshire

First published 1981
Third Impression 1982

British Library Cataloguing in Publication Data

Hunt, Janet
    The wholefood sweets book.
    1. Sweets – Recipes
    2. Natural foods – Recipes
    I. Title
    641.8'6   TX773

    ISBN 0-7225-0654-6
    ISBN 0-7225-0653-8 Pbk

Printed and bound in Great Britain

CONTENTS

INTRODUCTION

From childhood we are taught to associate sweets and sweet tasting foods with reward, with pleasure and with love. No wonder most people enjoy sweets in one form or another. To many it is those childhood favourites that get their mouths watering – sherbet, sugar mice, aniseed balls and bullseyes. Maybe the pictures they evoke of friendly corner sweet shops full of tall glass jars, of funfairs and circuses, seaside outings and Saturday morning pictures have something to do with it.

Others prefer their sweets in more sophisticated guises – chocolate mousse served elegantly in long, chilled glasses, tiny crisp and golden biscuits served with afternoon tea, or sizzling *crêpes* dusted with sugar, decorated with a twist of lemon. We tend to assume that we will automatically lose our love of sweet things as we grow up, but this seems to be far from the truth. In reality, we become more addicted to them than ever.

The Sweet Tooth is not, of course, a new thing. In ancient Britain it had to be satisfied with honey, the only sweetener generally available. Spices and dried fruits were also used, but few of the poorer folk had the chance of tasting anything sweet except the occasional piece of fruit.

Sweets and Tradition

It was George I who set the fashion for ending a meal with a sweet dish. His taste for heavy, rich and often indigestible puddings started a trend that was to earn the British the nickname of 'pudding eaters'. But by the end of the nineteenth century, the dessert (from the French 'desservir' – to clear the table) had expanded to include a variety of elaborate sweet dishes such as ices, preserves and cakes.

Sweets play a part in the traditions of other cultures, too. In India the Hindus prove their devotion to gods and goddesses with gifts of sweets, an offering that the Vedas scriptures assure them is well received. They also form an important part of their festivals, as do the sugar skulls that are sold in the streets on Mexico's Day of the Dead. In Italy, sugar almonds are thrown as part of the wedding ceremony. Also, most countries that celebrate Christmas do so with the aid of special sweets, cakes and biscuits that are as much part of the festivities as the church service and the family gathering.

In America, not so long ago, ice cream parlours were the heart of each small town, where young and old alike would gather in the soda-scented cool, fans whirring softly overhead, to eat ice creams with improbable flavours like vanilla-lime and sarsaparilla. Today more Americans go for yogurt, and with nearly thirty flavours to choose from, they need never be bored with it.

Think of France and you think of those spotless patisseries displaying row upon row of delicious pastries. In Greece they use honey frequently, producing such delights as paklava and honey cake, adding nuts to balance the sweetness. Flowers often find their way out of the garden and into the more traditional foods – the Chinese add chrysanthemum petals to flavour their sweets, while the Indians prefer the rose. (Not so long ago, the British too ate cooked primroses and drank gillyflower cordial, but today's cooks rarely use flowers, except for candying them as cake decoration).

So sweet foods are an important part of tradition. They are a way of expressing affection, and usually they are very pleasurable to eat. But do they have any part to play in the diet of a wholefooder? Can eating sweets ever be compatible with eating for health?

Eating for Health

Generally, of course, the answer is no. Most of the manufactured sweet foods available in this country today contain ingredients that are dubious if not positively harmful – refined white sugar, colourings, flavourings, preservatives (none of these have one iota of nutritional value). White sugar, which tends to be used in huge amounts in many sweet foods (probably because it is relatively cheap), is now recognized as a major cause of a variety of health problems including diabetes, allergies, tooth decay, thrombosis, obesity, ulcers, and some cancers – and that is just a start.

Most of the additives used are chemically based, and the build-up effects they can have on the human body are still not fully known. All that *is* known is that natural foods put less strain on the system, supply more benefits, and usually taste better. When you consider that the British consume more sweets, per head, than anyone else in the world, and that the majority of these sweets are bought over the counter, it is easy to understand why the National Health Service is under such strain.

None of this means you have to deprive yourself or your children of the pleasure of sweet foods. Make your own at home and you can decide exactly what goes into them – and what you would prefer to leave out! Most recipes can be adapted to include wholefoods. Raw brown sugar can replace white; low cholesterol margarine can replace at least some of the high fat butter. Junky decorative ingredients can be left out and you can increase the food value of your sweets by adding nuts, dried fruits and honey. Shop-bought sweets will, of course, last forever – yours will not. But, surely, it is better to eat them freshly made and know that you are getting the maximum food value? Treat your sweet-making sessions as an entertainment, perhaps get the family to help you, and experiment with different recipes from time to time. Make small amounts, and look forward to your next session.

You can switch ingredients in other sweet foods too. Ice creams, jams, desserts, biscuits, can all be transformed from empty foods into wholefoods that are more satisfying, tastier, and safer to eat. And if they really are too 'more-ish', you can have an extra portion without feeling too guilty.

It must be said that no-one who is aiming to live, for whatever reason, on a wholefood diet, should indulge their sweet tooth too often. With the recipes given in this book you can be confident in the knowledge that your sweet treat does contain some food value. But if sweet treats are treated as the bulk of your diet, you will be missing out on other valuable nutrients that can only be obtained from such items as salads, fresh vegetables and fruits. Balance out your diet with care. You will know when you have got it right by the way you feel. If you want to make sweet foods part of that diet, go right ahead and do so. Just make sure that they are as close to wholefoods as possible – and that you don't let them take over. Remember the saying 'A little of what you fancy does you good'; then remember – a little!

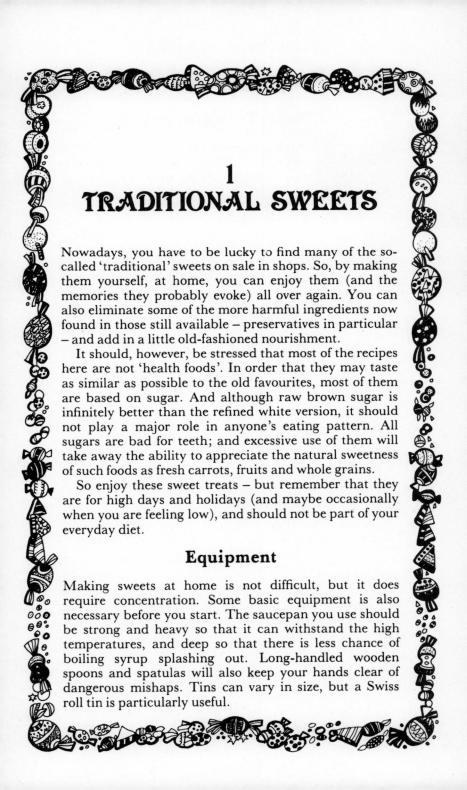

1
TRADITIONAL SWEETS

Nowadays, you have to be lucky to find many of the so-called 'traditional' sweets on sale in shops. So, by making them yourself, at home, you can enjoy them (and the memories they probably evoke) all over again. You can also eliminate some of the more harmful ingredients now found in those still available – preservatives in particular – and add in a little old-fashioned nourishment.

It should, however, be stressed that most of the recipes here are not 'health foods'. In order that they may taste as similar as possible to the old favourites, most of them are based on sugar. And although raw brown sugar is infinitely better than the refined white version, it should not play a major role in anyone's eating pattern. All sugars are bad for teeth; and excessive use of them will take away the ability to appreciate the natural sweetness of such foods as fresh carrots, fruits and whole grains.

So enjoy these sweet treats – but remember that they are for high days and holidays (and maybe occasionally when you are feeling low), and should not be part of your everyday diet.

Equipment

Making sweets at home is not difficult, but it does require concentration. Some basic equipment is also necessary before you start. The saucepan you use should be strong and heavy so that it can withstand the high temperatures, and deep so that there is less chance of boiling syrup splashing out. Long-handled wooden spoons and spatulas will also keep your hands clear of dangerous mishaps. Tins can vary in size, but a Swiss roll tin is particularly useful.

Sugar Temperatures

Many of the recipes given here are for uncooked sweets. When making sweets by boiling sugar, it is important to judge the precise temperature at which to stop the heating process. The easiest way to do this is with a sugar thermometer, which is well worth investing in if you intend to make sweets fairly frequently. An alternative way to judge the temperature is by dropping a small quantity of syrup into a bowl of cold water, and noting its reaction. When doing this, always remove the saucepan from the heat so that the syrup does not go past setting point.

The stages through which the sugar will go when dropped into cold water are:

Smooth – 220°F/105°C. Sugar will cling to fingers in a sticky film.

Soft ball – 237°F/114°C. Forms a soft ball when rolled between fingers.

Firm ball – 247°F/119°C. Forms a firm but pliable ball.

Soft crack – 280°F/137°C. Separates into threads which break quite easily.

Hard crack – 310°F/154°C. Separates into threads which are hard and brittle.

Caramel – 340°F/171°C. Sugar goes much darker; be careful not to overcook or the mixture will taste burnt.

Sugar should always be dissolved at a low temperature, and use a wooden spoon to stir it, making sure that no granules remain. Then bring the syrup to the boil, and, unless otherwise stated, do not stir again.

Ingredients

Ingredients are given for each recipe, but you can adapt them as you wish. For example, butter is high in cholesterol. Soft margarines are preferable nutritionally, but may not be absorbed properly, which may affect the results. The decision is up to you (a compromise being to use half and half). Use the milk you prefer, when called for, and remember that you can make any milk creamier by adding extra skimmed milk powder. If you use cider vinegar instead of malt, use less than indicated as its taste tends to be stronger.

None of these sweets contain the preservatives that formed part of many traditional recipes, and they therefore will not keep as well. Enjoy them when they are fresh – and enjoy making another batch when you want some more. Smaller batches will in any case, help you resist the temptation to overeat.

Finally, children often enjoy making sweets, and there is no reason why they should not help you. Choose those recipes that need no cooking preferably, and if boiling syrups are involved, keep a close watch on things.

Honeycomb

2 oz (50g) margarine
12 oz (350g) brown sugar
6 tablespoonsful honey
4 tablespoonsful water
2 teaspoonsful bicarbonate of soda
1 teaspoonful vinegar

Combine the margarine, sugar, honey, vinegar and water in a saucepan. Heat gently and stir until the sugar has completely dissolved, then bring to boil and continue boiling until syrup reaches 280°F/137°C (soft crack stage). Remove from the heat, and stir in the bicarbonate of soda, then pour immediately into a small ready-greased tin. The bicarbonate of soda will act to make the syrup froth up and produce that famous honeycomb texture. Leave to cool and set. Break into uneven pieces.

Fondants

**8 oz (225g) brown sugar, powdered in grinder
1 egg white
1 dessertspoonful lemon juice
1-2 tablespoonsful double cream – optional
1 oz (25g) hazelnuts – optional**

Whisk the egg white briefly. Using a spoon, beat in the sugar and lemon juice, and continue doing so until the fondant is firm enough to hold its shape. For a smoother taste, beat in a little cream.

Roll out the fondant on a sugared board and cut into the desired shapes, i.e. circles, crescents, triangles. Top with nuts, if you are using them. Leave to harden.

Variations
1. Add 2 oz (50g) of coconut to the fondant mixture.
2. Add a little peppermint essence for peppermint creams.
3. Add finely chopped preserved ginger and a teaspoonful of ground ginger.
4. Omit the lemon juice; use rose water instead.
5. Try almond essence, with an almond decorating each sweet.
6. Instead of rolling fondant out, shape it into balls with a hazelnut tucked in the centre.

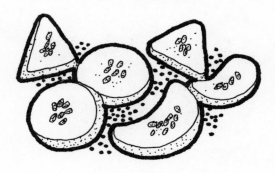

Nut Brittle

6 oz (175g) brown sugar
4 oz (100g) roasted cashew nuts
Pinch of bicarbonate of soda

Put the sugar into a saucepan on a low heat, and keep stirring until it melts. Continue cooking until it reaches 310°F/154°C (hard crack stage). Remove from heat. Add the bicarbonate of soda and nuts and stir briefly. Pour in as thin a sheet as possible onto a ready-greased baking tray. Leave to cool and harden; break into uneven pieces.

Alternatively, you can simply turn the mixture onto the baking sheet, and leave it to cool just enough to handle. Then use your hands to pull it apart into rough clusters of nuts and toffee.

Variations
Use any nuts you have handy. Larger ones, like brazil nuts, should be chopped into small pieces. Coconut chunks are also good in brittle. For a smoother version, try making it with nuts that have been ground fine.

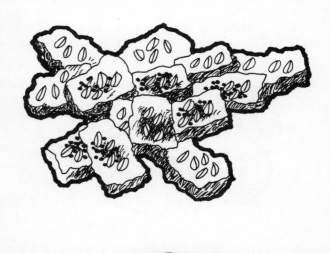

Lemon Sugar Twists

Rind of 1 lemon
1 lb (450g) brown sugar
1 tablespoonful lemon juice
¼ pint (150ml) water

Chop the lemon rind into rough pieces, then put it with the other ingredients into a saucepan. Heat gently, stirring until the sugar dissolves, then bring to the boil. Continue cooking until 280°F/140°C (soft crack stage), then remove the lemon rind and take saucepan from the heat. Oil a shallow tin and pour in the syrup. When it firms up a little, cut into strips (with oiled scissors), twist, and leave to set hard.

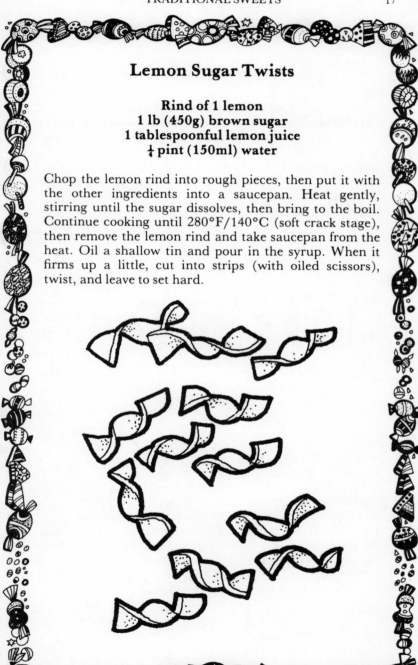

Marzipan (1)

8 oz (225g) ground almonds
2 tablespoonsful honey (preferably the solid variety)
Orange flower water to taste

Simply knead all the ingredients together until you have a firm, smooth paste. Roll this out and cut into simple shapes. Alternatively, use to stuff dates and prunes, or sandwich together two walnuts. Marzipan can also, of course, be used to coat and decorate cakes.

Marzipan (2)

8 oz (225g) ground almonds
8 oz (225g) brown sugar, powdered in grinder
1 egg white
Almond essence

Mix together the almonds and sugar, and bind with the lightly beaten egg white. Add a few drops of almond essence, then knead to make a stiff dough.

Petits Fours

Use marzipan made in either of the ways given above, although the second recipe may be a little easier to handle. Shape into a variety of fruits, and paint with appropriate vegetable colouring. For example: make larger balls for oranges, pit surface with the fine part of a grater, use cloves as calyxes. Smaller balls can be rolled in sugar to give the bumpy look of raspberries and strawberries. Tiny balls can be pushed together to form a cluster of grapes. Serve *petits fours* in paper cases.

Fruit and Nut Chocolates

4 oz (100g) plain or milk chocolate
2 oz (50g) roasted hazelnuts
2 oz (50g) raisins

Break the chocolate into small pieces and put into a basin over a pan of boiling water. Stir until completely melted. Chop the fruit and nuts coarsely and mix into the chocolate. making sure everything is well coated. Use a spoon to drop small amounts of the mixture into paper cases. Leave to set.

Variations
Try walnuts, peanuts, brazil nuts, cashew nuts, sultanas, currants, apricots, etc. Most nuts and dried fruits go well with chocolate.

Coconut Ice

1 lb (450g) brown sugar
¼ pint (150ml) milk
4 oz (100g) desiccated coconut

Pour the milk into a thick saucepan, add the sugar, and bring slowly to the boil whilst stirring continually with a wooden spoon. When the mixture starts to boil, lower the heat and continue to boil it – without stirring – for 10 to 15 minutes, until it reaches 237°F/114°C (soft ball stage). Remove from the heat immediately, and stir in the desiccated coconut, making sure it is well distributed.

Pour immediately into a ready-greased shallow tin and use a knife to smooth the top. Leave to set before cutting into squares.

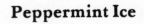

Peppermint Ice

Make as above, but substitute water for milk. Boil until syrup reaches 247°F/119°C (firm ball stage). Add 1 teaspoonful peppermint essence instead of coconut. Stir well, pour into tin.

Economy Fruit Fudge

1 lb (450g) brown sugar
2 oz (50g) margarine
½ pint (275ml) milk
4 oz (100g) raisins

Combine the sugar, margarine and milk in a saucepan and heat gently until the sugar dissolves, stirring frequently. Boil to a temperature of 237°F/114°C (soft ball stage), stirring occasionally, then add the fruit. Take off the heat and beat the mixture until smooth and thick. Pour into a ready-greased tin, and cut into squares when nearly set.

This fudge, although not as rich as the traditional kind, still tastes good. However, it will not keep for very long, so is best made in small amounts.

FRUIT FUDGE

Butterscotch

1 lb (450g) brown sugar
¼ pint (150ml) water
½ teaspoonful vanilla essence
2 oz (50g) butter

Put the sugar and water into a saucepan, and heat gently, stirring frequently, until the sugar dissolves. Bring to boil, and continue boiling to 280°F/137°C (soft crack stage). Stir in the essence, and then the butter, a portion at a time. When melted, pour the mixture in a small ready-greased tin. Mark into squares when cool, but do not break into pieces until completely cold.

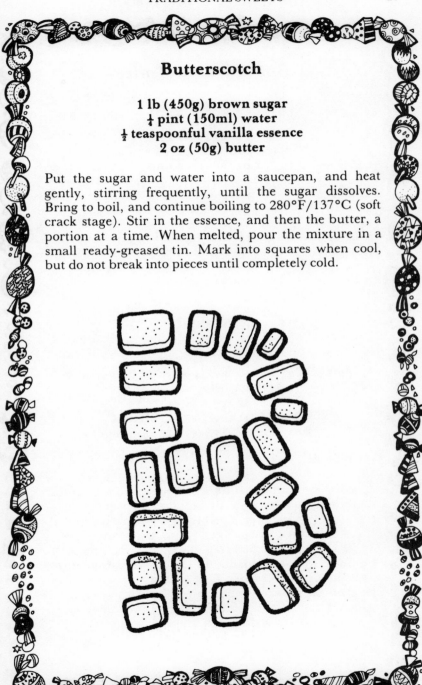

Honey Walnut Toffee

**8 oz (225g) honey
4 oz (100g) margarine
2 oz (50g) brown sugar
2 teaspoonsful mixed spice
2 oz (50g) walnuts**

Combine the honey and sugar in a saucepan; heat gently and stir until sugar dissolves. Add the margarine, stir again, then boil until reaching 280°F/137°C (soft crack stage). Take from heat and sprinkle in nuts and spices, mix thoroughly, then turn into a ready-greased tin. Leave in cool to firm up, mark into squares with a knife when half-set; break when completely cold.

Nougat

**4 oz (100g) honey
4 oz (100g) brown sugar, powdered in grinder
4 oz (100g) roasted almonds
2 egg whites
2 oz (50g) angelica or sultanas
2 oz (50g) _glacé_ cherries – optional
Rice paper**

Chop the nuts, the cherries and angelica. (Cherries and angelica are traditional ingredients in nougat, but for a more nutritious version use sultanas). Heat the honey, sugar and egg whites together in a saucepan until the sugar dissolves. Cook gently to a temperature of 247°F/119°C (firm ball stage), when the mixture should be thick and smooth. Stir in the nut and fruit pieces, distributing them evenly. Line a tin with rice paper and pour on the mixture, then top with another sheet of rice paper. Press down with a weight and allow to set thoroughly before cutting into squares.

Honey Fudge

2 oz (50g) margarine
2 tablespoonsful honey
1 lb (450g) brown sugar
4 tablespoonsful water
¼ pint (150ml) creamy milk (or ordinary milk plus 2 tablespoonsful skimmed-milk powder)
2 oz (50g) brazil nuts

Heat the margarine, honey, sugar, water and milk together gently until the sugar dissolves. Bring the syrup to the boil, and continue boiling for approximately 10 minutes, until it reaches 237°F/114°C (soft ball stage). Set aside for a short time, then beat hard with a wooden spoon until the mixture thickens before pouring it into a ready-greased tin. When half-set, chop the brazil nuts roughly, then sprinkle them over the fudge and press in lightly. Cut into squares when set.

Variations
1. Most nuts go well with fudge, so try other varieties.
2. Instead of nuts, add 2-3 tablespoonsful desiccated coconut.
3. For pineapple fudge, add 3 tablespoonsful crushed drained pineapple and ¼ teaspoonful lemon essence.
4. For orange or lemon fudge, add some grated rind and a little juice.
5. Chopped figs or dates go well with fudge.
6. An unusual taste comes from adding a few drops of cinnamon oil.
7. Peppermint oil makes peppermint fudge.

Buttermilk Toffee

$\frac{1}{4}$ pint (150ml) buttermilk
1 lb (450g) brown sugar
1 oz (25g) margarine
Vanilla essence

Place sugar in a saucepan together with just enough buttermilk to cover it. Heat gently, stirring, until the sugar dissolves, then add the margarine and bring the mixture to the boil. Continue boiling for about 30 minutes, stir in the essence, and remove from the heat. Pour into a ready-greased tin and leave to harden. Mark into squares when half-set.

Brown Sugar Mice

1 lb (450g) brown sugar, powdered in grinder
2 tablespoonsful honey
1 egg white
Currants
String

Put most of the sugar into a bowl, and use a wooden spoon to stir in the egg white. Add enough honey to make the mixture firm so that it can be shaped. Form into 8 mice, moulding the ears carefully. Use the currants to make eyes, and add a short length of string to each mouse for a tail. Leave to dry.

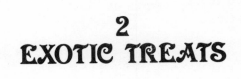

2
EXOTIC TREATS

Sweets do not have to be traditional, nor do they have to be made to appeal to younger palates. There is no reason why sweets should not change, as have so many of the foods we eat today, into a new food satisfying the tastes of a whole new group of people.

Sweets with a Difference

If you would like to try something completely different, there are many ways in which you can do so. With a little imagination, many of the old kinds of sweets can be adapted to produce exciting new tastes and textures. The secret is to be brave and put those wild ideas into practice. The results will probably taste nothing like you expect, but delicious just the same – and that is what creative cookery is all about.

Besides new versions of old favourites, try some of the sweetmeats that may be traditional in other parts of the world, but are less familiar in this country. Indian halvahs, for example are delicately flavoured – they also, because of their unusual ingredients, have a lot of natural goodness in them.

Then there are those sweets that appeal to adults rather than children; more unusual varieties, not so much for munching whilst rambling, but for nibbling elegantly after a meal, over coffee and conversation – sophisticated sweets.

These, and many more sweets, can be made at home. Some are complicated and take longer; others require more exotic ingredients and techniques. (You might also

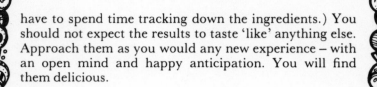

have to spend time tracking down the ingredients.) You should not expect the results to taste 'like' anything else. Approach them as you would any new experience – with an open mind and happy anticipation. You will find them delicious.

Ginger Biscuit Fudge

6 oz (175g) ginger biscuit crumbs
2 oz (50g) margarine
2 oz (50g) honey
2 oz (50g) brown sugar
1-2 teaspoonsful ginger

Melt the margarine in a saucepan, stir in the honey and sugar, heating gently until they dissolve and blend. Sprinkle in the ground ginger. Add the finely crushed crumbs, and mix so that they are well distributed through the syrup. Spoon into a greased tin, mark into squares and leave to set hard.

Variations
Use digestive biscuits instead of ginger, and a little vanilla essence instead of the powder. Finely crushed chocolate biscuits also make a tasty if unusual fudge.

Truffles

4 oz (100g) plain chocolate
2 oz (50g) margarine
2 egg yolks
2 oz (50g) ground almonds
4 oz (100g) brown sugar, powdered in grinder
Carob powder
Desiccated coconut

Break the chocolate into small pieces and melt it with the margarine in a basin over a saucepan of hot water. Remove from the heat and stir in the egg yolks; then add the ground almonds and sugar, working them into the mixture evenly. Turn onto a plate and leave somewhere cool to firm up. Shape into balls and roll in carob powder or coconut – or do half in one, half in the other.

Carrot Halvah

1 lb (450g) carrots
4 oz (100g) margarine
½ pint (275ml) milk
8 oz (225g) brown sugar
2 oz (50g) ground almonds
2 oz (50g) cashew nuts
1 teaspoonful rose water

Grate the carrots, then cook gently in the margarine for 10-15 minutes. Stir in the sugar. Pour on the milk and bring to the boil. Lower the heat, stir in the ground almonds and a teaspoonful rose water (or to taste), then cook until the mixture becomes thick. It will tend to stick to the saucepan, so stir it frequently and keep the heat low. When all the liquid has been absorbed, pour it into a Swiss roll tin that has first been rinsed in cold water. Smooth the surface, sprinkle with cashew nuts, and leave to cool. Cut into squares.

Coffee Candy

1 lb (450g) brown sugar
1 tablespoonful wholemeal flour
Just under ¼ pint (150ml) strong milky grain coffee

Stir the sifted flour into the coffee, combining them well, then put into a saucepan with the sugar. Heat gently, stirring to dissolve the sugar, then continue boiling for about 10 minutes. Pour into a ready-greased tin and leave to cool. Cut into bars when firm.

Praline

4 oz (100g) brown sugar
4 oz (100g) almonds with skins

In a saucepan gently heat sugar and nuts until sugar dissolves. (It will speed up the process if you powder the sugar in a grinder first, but this is not absolutely necessary). Continue cooking and stirring, with a metal spoon, until the sugar is dark brown and reaches 340°F/171°C (caramel stage). Put onto a greased baking tray to harden, then either break into lumps and eat as a sweet, or crush the praline to sprinkle over ice cream, fruit salad, or cake.

Almond Barfi

1 lb (450g) brown sugar
Just under 2 pints (1 litre) water
1 teaspoonful ground cardamom
1 dessertspoonful rose water
12 oz (350g) skimmed-milk powder
1-2 oz (25-50g) almonds

Prepare Swiss roll tin or similar by greasing lightly. Bring the sugar and water to the boil gently, stirring until the sugar dissolves completely. Then boil briskly for about 10 minutes, until the syrup reaches 237°F/114°C (soft ball stage). Remove from heat, and stir milk powder, cardamom and rose water in quickly, then turn at once into prepared tin. Smooth top, scatter on roughly chopped almonds and press them down lightly. Mark into squares, then leave to cool.

Traditionally, this is made with dried full-fat milk rather than the skimmed variety, and it does give a creamier tasting sweet. It is, however, higher in cholesterol – it is also difficult to find in shops. The choice is yours.

Molasses Toffee

2 oz (50g) margarine
2 oz (50g) butter
8 oz (225g) brown sugar
8 oz (225g) molasses

Melt margarine and butter in a saucepan, then stir in the sugar and heat until it dissolves. Add the molasses, blend well, then boil syrup, without stirring again, until it reaches 310°F/154°C (hard crack stage). Pour immediately into a ready-greased tin, and when set, cut into squares.

Candied Orange Peel

4 oranges
6 oz (175g) brown sugar
1 tablespoonful water
2 oz (50g) brown sugar, powdered in grinder

Carefully pare away the thin outer peel of each orange, cut into strips, and boil in water for 10-15 minutes. If any white pith remains on the peel it should now be quite easy to remove. In a saucepan heat the 6 oz (175g) brown sugar with the water, and stir until a syrup forms. Put the peel into this and simmer gently until it becomes transparent. This process can take anything up to an hour. Drain well, roll in the powdered sugar, and leave on a wire rack until completely dry. Keep in an airtight container.

Variation
Candied lemon and grapefruit peel can be made in the same way.

Sugared Brazil Nuts

6 oz (175g) container frozen concentrated orange juice
12 oz (350g) brown sugar
1 lb (450g) brazil nuts, shelled

Turn juice concentrate into a saucepan and stir in the sugar. Stir as you bring mixture to the boil, then continue boiling gently until temperature reaches 237°F/114°C (soft ball stage). Take syrup off the heat, mix in the nuts, and leave to cool, then stir again until mixture thickens. Use a spoon to separate the nuts, and drop them one at a time onto a greased baking sheet. Leave to become firm.

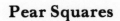

Pear Squares

**1 lb (450g) dried pears
2 lb (900g) brown sugar
Desiccated coconut**

Soak the pears until plump and soft, then remove any tough core, and mince the rest as finely as possible. Put the sugar and pear pieces into a saucepan and cook over a low heat for about an hour. The mixture will have a tendency to stick, so give it a good stir every now and again.

Rinse a Swiss roll tin in cold water and pour the pear mixture into it, sprinkle the top with coconut, and leave to cool. Cut into squares. Roll in more coconut if still sticky to handle.

Peppermint Delights

**Peppermint essence
1 lb (450g) brown sugar, powdered in grinder
2 oz (50g) margarine
2 tablespoonsful milk
2 oz (50g) chocolate
1 oz (25g) walnuts**

Melt the margarine, stir in the milk and essence, then work in the sugar a bit at a time until a smooth, heavy dough is formed. Use a rolling pin (plus a little skimmed-milk powder to help prevent sticking), roll peppermint dough out as thinly as possible. Cut into circles, diamonds, or whatever shape you prefer. Set aside to firm up.

Break the chocolate into pieces and melt in a bowl placed above a pan of boiling water. Use a spoon to spread a little of the slightly cooled liquid over each of the sweets, then top with half a walnut. Leave to cool.

Coconut Toffee

4 oz (100g) brown sugar
¼ pint (150ml) water
4 oz (100g) desiccated coconut
1 teaspoonful vanilla essence

Heat together the sugar and water, stirring often, until sugar dissolves. Bring to the boil, then continue to cook on a low heat for five more minutes. Add the vanilla essence and coconut and beat to combine well. Cook, still stirring frequently, until mixture leaves the sides of the saucepan. Pour into a tin that has been lightly greased, and leave to harden. Cut into squares.

Indian Soya Sweets

4 oz (100g) soya flour
½ pint (275ml) evaporated milk
1-2 oz (25-50g) brown sugar
2 oz (50g) pistachio nuts
2 tablespoonsful grated orange or lemon rind
Rose water – optional

Blend together the flour and milk, making sure there are no lumps, then pour into a saucepan. Add sugar to taste, chopped pistachio nuts, grated rind, and a few drops of rose water. Cook gently for 5 minutes, then pour into a container rinsed in cold water. Leave to set before cutting into squares.

This protein-rich sweet can be varied by adding different nuts, some raisins, and/or mint flavouring instead of rose water.

Marrons Glacés

**1 lb (450g) chestnuts, fresh or dried
1 lb (450g) brown sugar
¼ pint (150ml) water
Vanilla essence**

Prepare the chestnuts by either peeling and skinning them, or reconstituting them. Cook in boiling water for 10 minutes or so. Meanwhile, make a thick syrup by dissolving the sugar in the ¼ pint (150ml) of water, and bringing it to the boil. Drop the chestnuts into the syrup, add a little essence, and boil for 10 minutes. Turn off heat, remove chestnuts from liquid and leave them to drain overnight. The next day boil the same syrup, and add the chestnuts, simmering them gently. When the syrup sticks to them, once again drain the chestnuts on a rack overnight. They are now ready to eat, or pack in an airtight container.

Apricot Halvah

4 cardamom seeds
1 stick cinnamon
2 cloves
1½ pints (850ml) water
4-6 tablespoonsful honey
4 oz (100g) wholewheat semolina
4 oz (100g) dried apricots
1-2 tablespoonsful grated orange peel

Add the seeds, broken cinnamon stick and cloves to the water; boil for 10 minutes. Stir in the honey and simmer for a further 10 minutes. Strain liquid. Return to saucepan with the semolina and continue heating, stirring frequently, until mixture is thick and smooth. If it seems too thin, sprinkle in a little more semolina. When mixture is almost solid, and pulling away from the saucepan sides, take it off the heat and add the peel and finely chopped apricots. Turn into a rinsed shallow tin, smooth the top, and leave to go completely cold before cutting into squares.

Sesame Bonbons

6 oz (175g) sesame seeds, raw or roasted
8 oz (225g) brown sugar
1½ pints (850ml) water

Grease a shallow tin. Combine the sugar and water in a saucepan; boil gently until the sugar dissolves. Bring to brisk boil and continue to cook until syrup reaches 280°F/137°C (soft crack stage). Stir in the seeds and cook, still stirring, over a medium heat until the mixture leaves the sides of the saucepan. Turn at once into the prepared tin, level the surface and mark into small oblongs. When cool, cut apart and store in an airtight tin or jar. Bonbons can be wrapped individually – choose the paper carefully and they make an ideal gift.

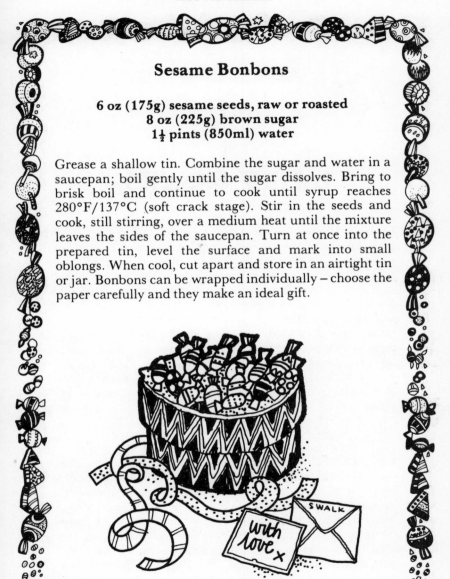

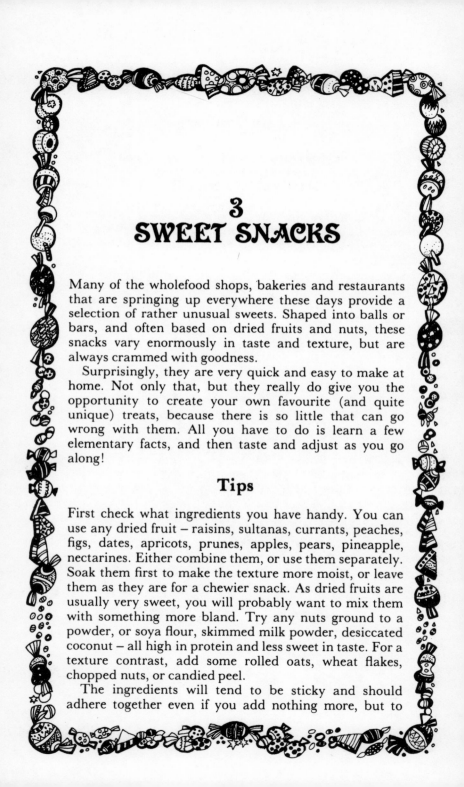

3
SWEET SNACKS

Many of the wholefood shops, bakeries and restaurants that are springing up everywhere these days provide a selection of rather unusual sweets. Shaped into balls or bars, and often based on dried fruits and nuts, these snacks vary enormously in taste and texture, but are always crammed with goodness.

Surprisingly, they are very quick and easy to make at home. Not only that, but they really do give you the opportunity to create your own favourite (and quite unique) treats, because there is so little that can go wrong with them. All you have to do is learn a few elementary facts, and then taste and adjust as you go along!

Tips

First check what ingredients you have handy. You can use any dried fruit – raisins, sultanas, currants, peaches, figs, dates, apricots, prunes, apples, pears, pineapple, nectarines. Either combine them, or use them separately. Soak them first to make the texture more moist, or leave them as they are for a chewier snack. As dried fruits are usually very sweet, you will probably want to mix them with something more bland. Try any nuts ground to a powder, or soya flour, skimmed milk powder, desiccated coconut – all high in protein and less sweet in taste. For a texture contrast, add some rolled oats, wheat flakes, chopped nuts, or candied peel.

The ingredients will tend to be sticky and should adhere together even if you add nothing more, but to ensure that the ball or bar will not crumble into pieces at the first bite, mix in a little lemon juice, some honey or molasses or margarine. Rose water or orange flower water go well with fruits that have more delicate flavours. Your choice depends on the main ingredients, and on how sweet you want your snack to be. You can also, of course, adjust the taste by sprinkling some spices into the mixture – cinnamon, ginger, coriander, cardamom.

When the mixing is done, you can press the resulting paste between sheets of edible rice paper and cut into bars. Doing it this way is especially preferable if the mixture tends to be excessively sticky.

If you want to make it into balls instead, use your hands to shape them, and then roll each one in a dry ingredient so that they do not stick together and are easy to handle – for example: wheat flakes, chopped or ground nuts, desiccated coconut, bran, toasted wheat germ, brown sugar, carob powder, soya flour, skimmed milk powder.

The one disadvantage of this kind of sweet is that, unlike the more traditional varieties, they will not keep for long, although a few days stored somewhere cool will not harm them. You can, of course, make them up in smaller batches as and when they are required.

Still on the subject of snacks, there is little to beat that old favourite – the fruit and nut mixture. Be imaginative in the fruit and nuts you combine, throw in a surprise or luxury ingredient, store the mixture in an airtight jar or tin. No-one in your house will have any excuse for eating empty foods when they feel a little empty.

Date and Walnut Balls

8 oz (225g) dates
4 oz (100g) walnuts
1 medium-sized apple
A little apple juice
½ teaspoonful coriander

Wash the dates, then chop them into very small pieces. Grate or mince the peeled, cored apple. Combine the dates and apple, stir in most of the coarsely chopped walnuts. Blend in the coriander. If the mixture is too dry, add some apple juice. Shape into balls and roll them in the remainder of the chopped walnuts. Set aside to firm up.

Spiced Apple Bran Bars

1 lb (450g) sweet apples
4 oz (100g) raisins
2 teaspoonsful mixed spice
Bran
Edible rice paper
1 tablespoonful honey – optional

Peel, core and chop apples, and cook with the spice and raisins in the minimum of water until soft. Drain off as much excess liquid as possible, then mix in sufficient bran to make a stiff mixture. Add honey if desired. Line a tin with the rice paper, spread the apple over it, top with another layer of paper. Press down evenly and leave to set. Cut into bars with a sharp knife.

Peanut Butter Slices

4 oz (100g) peanut butter
2-3 tablespoonsful skimmed-milk powder
3 oz (75g) raisins
2 tablespoonsful honey

Blend all ingredients together well, using enough milk powder to make a stiff paste. Shape the mixture into a roll, wrap in clingfoil, and put in the refrigerator to chill. Cut into slices. If you prefer, you can omit the honey.

Fruit Truffles

9 oz (250g) sultanas, raisins, currants, or a mixture
3 oz (75g) finely chopped nuts
3 oz (75g) wholemeal cakecrumbs
3 tablespoonsful milk
desiccated coconut

Wash the dried fruit, pat dry, then chop finely or put through a mincer. Combine the fruit, nuts and cakecrumbs in a bowl, pour on the milk and mix well. Set aside for at least an hour until the milk has been soaked up. Form the mixture into balls and roll in coconut. Put into paper cases.

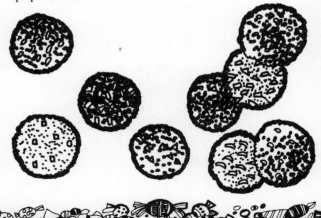

Candied Peel Cakes

3 oz (75g) candied peel
2 oz (50g) soya flour
3 oz (75g) desiccated coconut
2-3 teaspoonsful honey
Pinch cardamom powder
Edible rice paper

Chop the peel into small pieces, then mix with the honey, most of the coconut, soya flour and cardamom. Mixture should be firm enough to roll into balls. If it is too wet, add more soya flour; if too dry, stir in extra honey. Flatten the balls into round cakes and sandwich between two sheets of rice paper. Trim off the excess.

Muesli Crunch Bar

3 oz (75g) margarine
8 oz (225g) muesli
2 oz (50g) dried apple

Chop the apple into small pieces. Melt the margarine in a saucepan and stir in the muesli, blending the ingredients well. Take off the heat and add the apple pieces. Tip into a lightly greased shallow tin, press down firmly, and smooth the top with a knife, and mark into bars. Leave to cool before cutting.

Pear and Peanut Bars

4 oz (100g) dried pears
2 oz (50g) ground peanuts
1 oz (25g) roasted peanuts
1 tablespoonful honey or lemon juice
Edible rice paper

Wash, then chop the pears into small pieces, or mince them. Mix together with the ground peanuts and honey or lemon juice until the mixture is soft and sticky. Stir in the chopped roasted peanuts, distributing them evenly. Put a sheet of rice paper in the bottom of a tin, top with the pear and peanut mixture, then cover with more rice paper. Press down so that the surface is even. Leave to firm up before cutting into bars.

Mocha Nut Bites

4 oz (100g) hazelnuts
2 oz (50g) margarine
3 squares of chocolate
2 oz (50g) brown sugar, powdered in grinder
3 oz (75g) skimmed-milk powder
1 oz (25g) instant or grain coffee powder
1 oz (25g) carob powder

Roast the hazelnuts until pale gold, then grind them. Blend together the margarine and finely grated chocolate. Add the nuts and sugar; mix well. Sift the powdered milk and add to the other ingredients. So that the mixture is sticky enough to make into balls, you may have to knead it a little first. When shaped, roll each ball in the mocha powder (coffee and carob sifted together). Leave to become firm.

Tahini Treats

6 oz (175g) tahini (sesame spread)
3 tablespoonsful honey
3 oz (75g) sesame seeds
3 oz (75g) raisins
1 teaspoonful vanilla essence
3 oz (75g) toasted wheat germ
Millet flakes – optional

Blend together the tahini and honey, and stir in the vanilla. Add the seeds and raisins. Thicken the mixture with the wheat germ. Divide into small pieces, shape into balls and roll in millet flakes. Leave in refrigerator to chill.

Milk and Honey Bars

3 oz (75g) dried figs
3 oz (75g) ground almonds
6 oz (175g) skimmed milk powder
½ teaspoonful cardamom powder
2 tablespoonsful honey
Edible rice paper

Chop the washed figs as fine as possible. Mix the almond and powdered milk together until well blended and then add the figs and cardamom powder. Use the honey to bind the mixture. Press between two sheets of rice paper and leave to harden a little. Cut into bars.

Stuffed Dates

20 well-shaped dried dates
4 brazil nuts
8 hazelnuts
Small square marzipan
2 oz (50g) desiccated coconut
1 tablespoonful honey
1 oz (25g) cream cheese

Wash the dates, pat dry, then carefully cut them open and remove the stones. Use the brazil nuts to stuff four of the dates, and put two hazelnuts in each of four more. Cut the marzipan into four and use each piece to stuff another date. Blend the coconut with the honey and share the mixture between four more dates, and fill the remaining ones with a portion of cream cheese each. Eat fairly soon after preparing these sweets.

Apricot and Coconut Balls

4 oz (100g) dried apricots
4 tablespoonsful honey
3 tablespoonsful margarine
5 oz (150g) desiccated coconut
Soya flour

Soak the apricot pieces in water until soft, then drain and chop into small pieces. Combine the honey and margarine, and beat until smooth, then add the apricot pieces and most of the coconut. When well blended, stir in enough soya flour to make the mixture fairly dry and easy to handle.

Divide into pieces about the size of an apricot and shape into balls, then roll in the remainder of the desiccated coconut.

Maple Granola

8 oz (225g) pure maple syrup
2-3 tablespoonsful oil
4 oz (100g) wholewheat flakes
12 oz (350g) rolled oats
4 oz (100g) wheat germ
4 oz (100g) sesame seeds
4 oz (100g) desiccated coconut

Heat the oil and syrup in a heavy saucepan; tip in the oats and wheat flakes, stirring to make sure they are coated with the syrup mixture. After cooking them gently, stirring occasionally, for 15-20 minutes, add the rest of the ingredients. Continue cooking the granola for 5-10 minutes longer, until golden in colour. Remove from heat, leave to cool, then store in an airtight tin or jar.

This sweet, crunchy granola can be eaten by the handful, just as it is. Try it, too, as a breakfast cereal with milk, or a dessert with creamy yogurt, fresh or dried fruit. It can also be used as a crumble topping, or with ice cream.

Banana Crisps

8 large firm bananas

Remove the skins, then carefully cut each banana into wafer-thin slices, and lay on baking sheets so that they do not touch or overlap. Cook in a very slow oven 225°F/110°C (Gas Mark ¼) for 1-2 hours, until they become dry and crackly, like potato crisps.

Allow to cool, then store in an airtight tin or jar.

California Mix

2 oz (50g) banana crisps (see previous recipe)
2 oz (50g) dried pineapple
2 oz (50g) dried apricots
2 oz (50g) dates
2 oz (50g) raisins
1 oz (25g) cashew nuts
1 oz (25g) hazelnuts
1 oz (25g) walnuts
1 oz (25g) flaked almonds
1 oz (25g) pumpkin seeds
2 oz (50g) desiccated or flaked coconut

Chop the dried fruit into smallish pieces; do the same with the cashew nuts, walnuts and hazelnuts. Combine all the ingredients and store in an airtight tin or jar. Makes an ideal snack as it is high in natural sugars and protein.

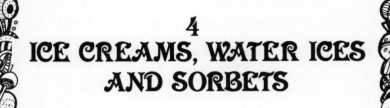

4
ICE CREAMS, WATER ICES AND SORBETS

Despite our climate, ices are becoming increasingly popular in this country, as a sophisticated dessert for adults as well as being a favourite treat with children. But commercially made ice cream leaves a lot to be desired. To start with, it rarely contains cream – 90 per cent of British ice creams use vegetable oil instead of cream. If you think that makes it sound a healthier product, think again. The British Nutrition Foundation claims there is more fat in non-dairy ice cream – around 8.2 grams (just over $\frac{1}{4}$ oz) per scoop. Ice cream is also, of course, rich in white sugar, artificial flavourings and colourings.

But that is only half the story. The other half of your commercially made family brick is likely to be made up of air. There may be little to complain about from a health viewpoint, but as ice cream sells by volume rather than weight, it can be very expensive air.

Making Your Own

Home-made ices are more nutritious, cheaper, and not at all difficult to make once you have mastered a few basic rules. They can also be varied *ad infinitum* – with different ingredients, flavourings and combinations. You and your family will never grow tired of ices once you have started to make your own, and it is good to know you can indulge *and* get real nutritional value at the same time.

Ices can be made in the ice-making compartment of a refrigerator or in a deep freeze. Use freezing trays or any metal tins or moulds. For ice cream it is important to freeze the ingredients as quickly as possible, so turn the controls to the lowest setting at least half an hour before you make up the mixture. Once it has frozen firm, you can turn the setting back to normal. Although such fast-freezing is not strictly necessary with water ices and sorbets, it will do no harm. (Sorbets, incidentally, are simply water ices with a high proportion of egg whites added). When serving ices, always chill the glasses or bowls.

Texture

To improve the texture of home-made ices (which can be a little gritty compared with the commercially made variety), most of them should be beaten or stirred when half set, and then refrozen. This breaks down the crystals and adds air (and bulk) to the mixture. Do not, however, reduce them to liquid.

For a creamy result, it is necessary to use a mixture that is sufficiently rich in fat. Double cream is often recommended in small quantities. Whipping cream is a good alternative – if you cannot buy it, make your own by combining equal quantities of single and double cream. Evaporated milk can also be used, or make single cream thicker (and more nutritious) by adding skimmed milk powder. Take great care not to over-beat double cream or it will become rather solid and buttery. When the whisk leaves a mark on the cream, it is ready to use.

Sugar should be used in limited amounts as it can hinder freezing. Grind brown sugar if it is not dissolved first, to give a smoother texture to the ice. Honey is ideal – it also has a strong unique flavour, which is important as freezing tends to diminish the sweetness and flavour of the ingredients.

None of the recipes given here include colouring. Many of them will, in fact, have a natural tint from the ingredients, but if you wish to add more colours, use appropriate vegetable colourings before freezing the mixture. It will tend to be paler when frozen, so adjust the colouring accordingly.

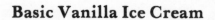

Basic Vanilla Ice Cream

2 egg yolks
2 oz (50g) brown sugar
¼ pint (150ml) milk
1 teaspoonful vanilla essence
⅓ pint (200ml) double cream

Use a double saucepan (or a bowl over a pan of hot water) in which to combine the egg yolks and sugar, stirring well with a wooden spoon. Boil the milk and pour it over the yolks, still stirring, and continue to stir over the heat until the custard coats the back of the spoon. Set the mixture aside to cool, stir in the vanilla essence. Whip the double cream and fold it into the custard. Pour into the freezing tray and freeze until it begins to set around the edges. Turn ice cream into a cold bowl, beat again, and return to freezing tray. Leave to set solid.

Variations

1. Add 2 oz (50g) desiccated coconut to the above recipe.
2. Add chopped preserved ginger to the above recipe.
3. Use almond essence instead of vanilla; add chopped roast almonds.
4. Use peppermint essence instead of vanilla.
5. Omit essence – add 2 oz (50g) chopped pistachio nuts and 1 teaspoonful rose water.
6. Omit essence – mix 2 oz (50g) instant coffee in 2 tablespoonsful of milk and add to mixture.
7. Omit essence – mix 2 oz (50g) cocoa in 2 tablespoonsful of milk and add to mixture.
8. Omit essence – mix 2 oz (50g) carob powder in 2 tablespoonsful of milk and add to mixture.
9. Omit essence – add 1 lb (450g) soft fruit *purée* (sieve to remove pips).

Dried Apricot Ice Cream

8 oz (225g) dried apricots
2 tablespoonsful orange juice
2 oz (50g) honey – optional
¼ pint (150ml) single cream
¼ pint (150ml) double cream

Soak the apricots, then simmer gently until well cooked. Drain, then make a *purée* of the fruit by putting it through a sieve, mashing it, or by using a blender. Combine the *purée* with the orange juice, honey and single cream, and pour into freezing tray. Leave until half frozen.

Whip the double cream lightly. Remove the fruit from the freezer, turn into a bowl, and whip just long enough to break up the crystals, then stir in the whipped double cream. Return to the freezing tray, and freeze until completely set.

Banana Ice Cream

4 large ripe bananas
½ pint (275ml) double or whipping cream
2 oz (50g) honey
1 tablespoonful lemon juice

Mash the bananas well, or *purée* them in a blender. Add the honey and lemon juice, stirring so that all the ingredients are thoroughly blended. Whip the cream until light and smooth, then fold it into the banana mixture. Pour into freezing tray and leave until nearly firm, then tip into a mixing bowl and beat until frothy. Return to freezer until it is set.

Butter Pecan Ice Cream

3 oz (75g) pecan nuts,* coarsely chopped
2 oz (50g) butter
1½ tablespoonsful cornflour
5 oz (150g) brown sugar
½ pint (275ml) milk
¼ pint (150ml) double cream
1 teaspoonful vanilla essence

Combine the cornflour, sugar and milk, and cook gently until mixture thickens. You will need to stir it constantly to prevent sticking and burning. Take from the heat, add the vanilla essence, and leave to chill in the refrigerator. Meanwhile, cook the nuts lightly in the butter until just turning golden. Whip the cream until stiff, then stir in the nuts, and also the chilled mixture, combining all the ingredients well but gently. Pour into freezing tray and freeze until firm.

CLIVE BIRCH

*If Pecan nuts are unobtainable, walnuts have a similar taste and texture.

Russian Ice Cream

4 oz (100g) finely chopped candied peel
½ pint (275ml) double cream
1 oz (25g) brown sugar, powdered in grinder
1 oz (25g) blanched almonds, lightly roasted
1 teaspoonful vanilla extract
½ teaspoonful almond extract

Leave the candied fruit to soak in the two extracts for 10-15 minutes. Whip the double cream in a chilled bowl until it thickens, then add the sugar, a spoonful at a time, continuing to beat the mixture until it just holds its shape. Fold in the fruit and crushed almonds, mixing well. Put into freezing tray, cover with foil. Freeze until set.

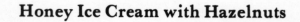

Honey Ice Cream with Hazelnuts

2 eggs
½ pint (275ml) milk
4 oz (100g) honey
1 teaspoonful vanilla essence
½ pint (275ml) whipping cream
3 oz (75g) roasted hazelnuts

Separate the eggs. In a saucepan gently heat the milk and egg yolks, stirring continually with a wooden spoon. When the mixture thickens enough to coat the spoon, add the honey and essence, and combine well. Cool, then freeze until the custard starts to set. Beat the whipping cream until light and airy, the egg whites until stiff. Fold them both into the custard carefully, along with the chopped hazelnuts. Freeze the ice cream until completely set.

Strawberry Yogurt Freeze

2 tablespoonsful honey
1 lb (450g) strawberries, fresh or frozen
¾ pint (425ml) natural yogurt

Clean the strawberries if fresh; defrost them if frozen. Mash the strawberries with the honey, retaining the juice if they are frozen. With fresh strawberries, add a spoonful or two of orange juice. Put the yogurt into a freezing tray and leave until mushy. Mix with strawberry *purée* and juice, and return to freezer until beginning to set. Beat again to lighten the mixture. Freeze until firm.

Marmalade Water Ice

1 lb (450g) marmalade (with thin peel)
1 tablespoonful orange juice
½ pint (275ml) water

Use a hand whisk or an electric blender to beat all ingredients together very thoroughly. Turn into freezing tray and freeze until the edges begin to set. Put the mixture into a cold bowl and beat until the ice crystals are broken down, but do not let it turn to liquid. Replace in freezer until set solid.

Variation
To make this into a delicious sorbet, add 2 whipped egg whites when you take the mixture from the freezer for the first time. Then refreeze.

Lemon Water Ice

1 pint (575ml) water
Grated rind of 1 lemon
4 oz (100g) honey
4 oz (100g) brown sugar
⅓ pint (200ml) lemon juice, freshly squeezed

Put the water, lemon rind, honey and sugar together in a saucepan, and heat gently, stirring to make sure the sugar dissolves completely. Then bring the liquid to the boil and continue boiling it for a further five minutes without stirring. Leave to cool. Then strain off the rind, pour in the lemon juice, and combine well. Turn the mixture into a freezing tray, and freeze until it is just beginning to stiffen. Whisk lightly, then refreeze.

Blackcurrant Water Ice

½ pint (275ml) water
½ teaspoonful agar agar
¼ pint (150ml) sweetened blackcurrant juice

Heat ¼ pint (150ml) of the water and whisk in the agar agar, making sure it dissolves completely. Cool. Add the rest of the water and the blackcurrant juice. Pour into freezing tray and freeze until mushy, then stir well before leaving the water ice to set.

Pineapple Sorbet

1 lb (450g) tin pineapple pieces in natural juice (or fresh equivalent)
1 lemon
Approx. ¼ pint (150ml) water
2 oz (50g) brown sugar
2 egg whites

Add sufficient water to the pineapple juice to make a total of ½ pint (275ml) of liquid. Put in a saucepan with lemon rind and juice, plus the sugar, and simmer gently for 10 minutes. Sieve to remove the rind. Crush the pineapple into a *purée*, either by hand or in a blender, and add to the syrup, mixing well. Turn into a freezing tray and leave in freezer until the mixture begins to set. Beat the egg whites and fold them into the fruit. Refreeze.

Variation
Other fruits can be substituted for pineapple – for example: raspberries, gooseberries, blackcurrants, peaches, etc.

SAUCES

Honey Sauce

4 oz (100g) honey
Juice and rind of 1 lemon
¼ pint (150ml) water

Combine all ingredients in a saucepan, and stir gently over a low heat until the honey dissolves. Use as it is, or strain to remove the rind.

Jam Sauce

4 oz (100g) jam
2 teaspoonsful lemon juice
½ tablespoonful cornflour
½ pint (275ml) water

Put a little of the water into a bowl and blend in the cornflour. Heat the rest of the water and, when boiling, pour it onto the cornflour, stirring to keep the mixture smooth. Return to the saucepan, bring to the boil stirring continually, and boil for five minutes more. Stir in the jam and lemon juice, and blend well.

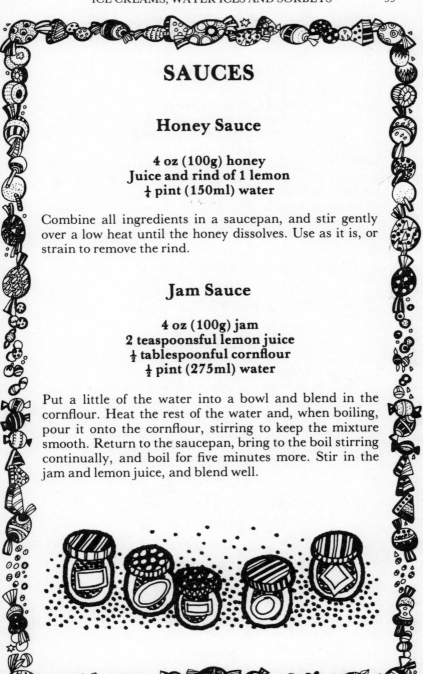

Caramel Sauce

1 oz (25g) margarine or butter
4 oz (100g) brown sugar
4-6 tablespoonful water

Melt the margarine in a pan; add the sugar and cook over a medium heat until it dissolves completely. Lower the heat and continue to stir the mixture until it boils, then remove from cooker. Add boiling water to the pan, a little at a time, stirring to keep the sauce smooth (any lumps can be removed by returning the pan to the heat so that they melt). Adjust the thickness of the sauce to the desired consistency by adding more or less water.

Chocolate Mint Sauce

3 oz (75g) plain chocolate
¼ pint (150ml) single cream
Approx. ¼ pint (150ml) milk
1-2 teaspoonful peppermint essence, to taste

Break the chocolate into small pieces and melt them gently over a pan of hot water. Add the cream and mix until the sauce is smooth. Flavour with peppermint essence. Thin with milk to the desired consistency.

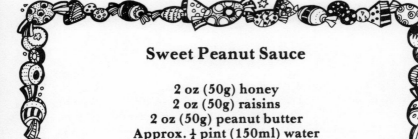

Sweet Peanut Sauce

2 oz (50g) honey
2 oz (50g) raisins
2 oz (50g) peanut butter
Approx. ¼ pint (150ml) water

Combine the water with the honey and raisins and boil for a few minutes, stirring to prevent sticking. Put the syrup and peanut butter together in a blender and beat until smooth. Add more water if you want a thinner sauce. Keep in fridge until needed.

Serving Suggestions

Ice creams and water ices made at home with wholesome ingredients taste delicious served just as they are – but do not forget to remove them from the freezer and leave in the fridge for at least an hour before eating, to get the full flavour.

For special occasions, however, they can be served in a variety of exciting ways. Parfaits, for example, are combinations of different flavoured ice creams and/or water ices, with fresh or cooked fruit, whipped cream, nuts and candied fruit. Here are some to try, then experiment with ideas of your own.

Cherry Parfait
Vanilla ice cream, stewed cherries, whipped cream.
Melon and Orange Parfait
Diced fresh melon with orange water ice, flaked toasted almonds.
Parfait Tutti-Frutti
Strawberry, chocolate and lemon ice cream with fruit salad.
Banana Chocolate Parfait
Banana ice cream with chocolate sauce, cream and nuts.
Apricot Parfait
Coffee ice cream with apricot water ice and stewed apricots.
Oranges and Lemons Parfait
Lemon water ice, orange ice cream with honey sauce.
Chestnut Parfait
Vanilla ice cream with chestnut compote and whipped cream.
Yogurt Parfait
Vanilla ice cream, fresh strawberries, natural yogurt and chopped nuts.

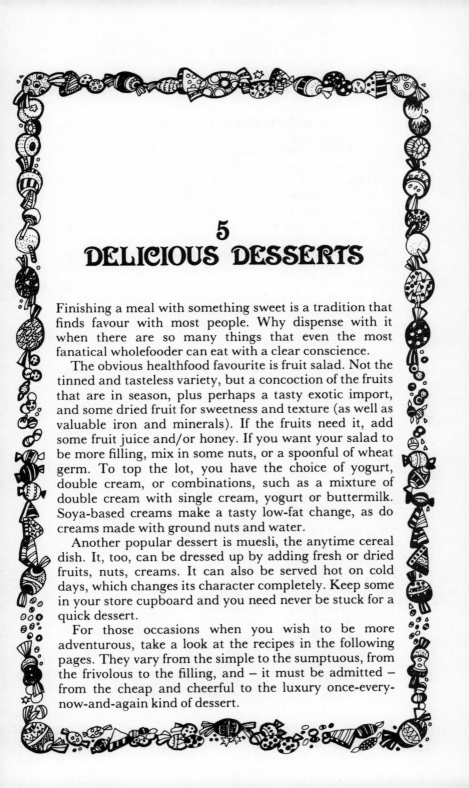

5
DELICIOUS DESSERTS

Finishing a meal with something sweet is a tradition that finds favour with most people. Why dispense with it when there are so many things that even the most fanatical wholefooder can eat with a clear conscience.

The obvious healthfood favourite is fruit salad. Not the tinned and tasteless variety, but a concoction of the fruits that are in season, plus perhaps a tasty exotic import, and some dried fruit for sweetness and texture (as well as valuable iron and minerals). If the fruits need it, add some fruit juice and/or honey. If you want your salad to be more filling, mix in some nuts, or a spoonful of wheat germ. To top the lot, you have the choice of yogurt, double cream, or combinations, such as a mixture of double cream with single cream, yogurt or buttermilk. Soya-based creams make a tasty low-fat change, as do creams made with ground nuts and water.

Another popular dessert is muesli, the anytime cereal dish. It, too, can be dressed up by adding fresh or dried fruits, nuts, creams. It can also be served hot on cold days, which changes its character completely. Keep some in your store cupboard and you need never be stuck for a quick dessert.

For those occasions when you wish to be more adventurous, take a look at the recipes in the following pages. They vary from the simple to the sumptuous, from the frivolous to the filling, and – it must be admitted – from the cheap and cheerful to the luxury once-every-now-and-again kind of dessert.

A Balanced Approach

What they have in common is the fact that most of their ingredients can be classified as either wholefoods or healthfoods. This is, of course, a generalization. Many traditional dishes tend to be made with refined sugar, flour, etc., and these have been adapted to incorporate the varieties that are known to be more nourishing. However, some of the original ingredients cannot be replaced or omitted without completely changing the taste and texture of the dish, and in these cases they have been retained. Assuming that you are unlikely to make most of the dishes part of your regular day-to-day eating pattern, such discrepancies will do little harm.

One such ingredient that crops up quite often is double cream. Its main claim to disrepute is that it is high in saturated fats, but if – like most people who choose their foods for health – you are vegetarian, or eat very little meat and dairy products, the occasional dessert treat will be unlikely to affect you. You can lower the fat level in almost all the recipes here by using half double and half single cream. Yogurt, of course, is the perfect substitute in those instances where the cream does not need to be whipped.

Finally, do take care to balance your meals. Many of the recipes given here are rich in protein and natural sugars: with them you should serve a light and easily digested main course. When your savoury dish is to play the leading role, finish your meal with fresh fruit, or a delicate dessert such as yogurt mousse or avocado whip.

Oat Cheesecake

For base
2 oz (50g) margarine
4 oz (100g) rolled oats
2 oz (50g) sugar

For filling
6 oz (175g) cream cheese
3 tablespoonsful honey
2 eggs
1 teaspoonful mixed spice
1 oz (25g) chopped walnuts

Melt the margarine and mix well with the rolled oats and sugar. Use to cover the base of a lightly greased flan dish, and press down firmly. Beat the honey and cream cheese until a smooth sauce is formed. Add the well-beaten eggs and spice. Pour the mixture into the prepared flan case and bake at 350°F/180°C (Gas Mark 4) for 30 minutes. Five minutes before cheesecake is due to be taken from the oven, scatter the chopped walnuts over the top.

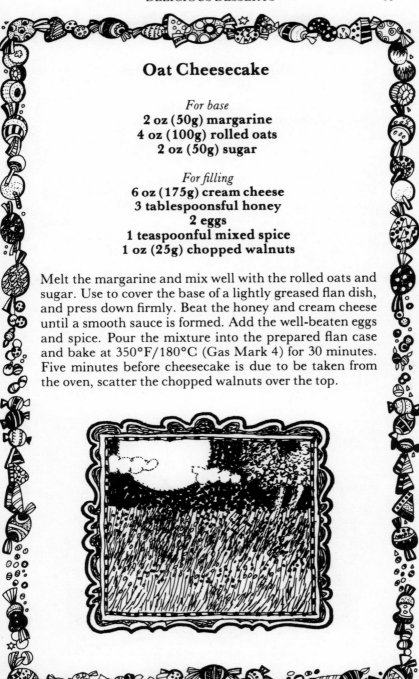

Baked Stuffed Apples

**4 large apples
4 tablespoonsful vegetarian mincemeat
1 oz (25g) margarine
Water or cider**

Wash and core the apples, then score the skin in a ring about half way down. Stuff a tablespoonful of mincemeat into each apple, place in a shallow baking dish, top with a knob of margarine. Pour a little liquid into the dish, and bake apples at 400°F/200°C (Gas Mark 6) for approximately 40 minutes. Baste occasionally with the liquid. Eat hot or cold.

Variations
Stuff apples with chopped dates mixed with coconut, raisins and nuts, or chopped dried peel; add honey or molasses for sweetening and, perhaps, a teaspoonful of spice for extra flavour. A higher protein dessert can be made by filling the apples with a mixture of nut butter and currants.

Apples wrapped in silver foil will cook more quickly and will mean less washing up.

Crème Caramel

**1 pint (575ml) milk
2 tablespoonsful skimmed milk powder
Finely grated rind of 1 lemon
4 eggs
7 oz (200g) brown sugar
1 teaspoonful vanilla essence
4 tablespoonsful water**

Combine the water and 4 oz (100g) of the sugar in a saucepan, stir until the sugar has dissolved, then cook gently until a golden brown caramel forms. Pour into a warmed *soufflé* dish and turn it around to coat the sides. Beat together the milk and milk powder, bring slowly to the boil, stir in the rest of the sugar. Cool for a few minutes, then add the well beaten eggs and mix thoroughly together with the vanilla essence and lemon rind. Pour into prepared *soufflé* dish, stand it in a baking tray of water. Bake at 350°F/180°C (Gas Mark 4) until set – approximately one hour. Cool, then chill before turning out onto a serving plate.

Coconut Apple Betty

2 oz (50g) margarine
6 oz (175g) wholemeal breadcrumbs
1½ lb (675g) apples
2 oz (50g) brown sugar
Grated rind and juice of ½ an orange
¼ pint (150ml) hot water
½-1 teaspoonful mixed spice
3 oz (75g) desiccated coconut
A little extra margarine

Melt the margarine, stir in the crumbs and coat evenly.
Peel and slice the apples. Layer the crumbs and apples in
a pie or *soufflé* dish, sprinkling each one with a little sugar,
rind, spice and coconut. End with breadcrumbs. Mix the
water and juice and pour over the dish, then add a final
sprinkling of coconut. Put margarine in tiny pieces on
top. Bake at 350°F/180°C (Gas Mark 4) for about three-
quarters of an hour, until apples are cooked and
breadcrumb topping turns golden.

Variation
Omit the coconut, and substitute sliced bananas for half of
the apple.

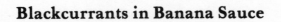

Blackcurrants in Banana Sauce

1 lb (450g) fresh or frozen blackcurrants
3 oz (75g) brown sugar
4 bananas
½ pint (275ml) single cream
2 tablespoonsful honey
2 tablespoonsful lemon juice

Wash and stem the blackcurrants; divide between four glasses. Sprinkle with sugar. Peel the bananas and cut into chunks. Put into a blender with the cream, honey and lemon juice, and beat until thick and smooth, then pour over the fruit.

Variation
Blend the bananas with 2-3 oz (50-75g) tofu soya bean curd. This results in a creamy, very high protein sauce that can also be used to fill a flan – add some dried fruit such as apricots, prunes, pears.

Marmalade Flan

Pastry to line an 8-inch flan dish (see page 76)
2 oz (50g) margarine
8 oz (225g) coarse peel marmalade
1 egg
2 oz (50g) raisins

Melt the margarine in a saucepan and stir in the
marmalade until it is melted, and well mixed with the
margarine. Remove from heat and leave to cool for a
short while before stirring in the beaten egg. Add raisins.
Pour the mixture into flan case. Bake at 400°F/200°C
(Gas Mark 6), then lower the heat to 350°F/180°C (Gas
Mark 4) and cook for 15 minutes longer, when filling
should be set. Eat hot or cold.

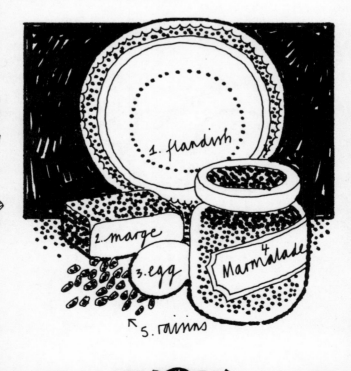

Yogurt Mousse

¼ pint (150ml) natural yogurt
2 egg whites
¾ pint (425ml) fruit *purée* (cooked or raw)
1 oz (25g) flaked toasted almonds

Blend together the yogurt and fruit, and put in the refrigerator to chill. Beat the egg whites until stiff, and stir them into the other ingredients. Divide mousse between 4 to 6 chilled glasses, and top each with a few of the almonds.

Nut and Honey Pizza

For dough
8 oz (225g) wholemeal flour
1 teaspoonful dried yeast
1 teaspoonful warm water
1 teaspoonful oil
⅛ pint (75ml) water

For topping
Approx. 3 tablespoonsful honey
3 oz (75g) coarsely chopped walnuts
1 teaspoonful mixed spice

Dissolve the yeast in the warm water and set aside. Mix the oil with the flour, and when the yeast mixture begins to froth, add it to the flour with the rest of the water. Knead until dough is smooth, then leave in a covered bowl in a warm place for one to two hours.

When the dough has risen, roll it into a thin circle, and spread over a well-greased baking sheet. Brush surface with a light film of oil, then spread with a good layer of honey, sprinkle on nuts and spices. Bake at 425°F/220°C (Gas Mark 7) for about 20 minutes.

Gooseberries with Millet

**1 lb (450g) gooseberries
Approx. 4 oz (100g) brown sugar or honey
4 oz (100g) cooked millet**

Cook the washed gooseberries with the sweetening and a little water until they form a moist *purée*. Combine with the cooked millet (which should be light and fluffy). Eat as it is, or with nuts and/or yogurt.

A quick and easy dessert that uses up left-over millet in a tasty way. Try it with other fruits, and if they are not juicy enough to coat the millet, add a little honey or orange juice.

Left-over cooked brown rice can be used up in the same way.

CLIVE BIRCH

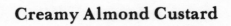

Creamy Almond Custard

1 pint (575ml) milk
2 tablespoonsful skimmed milk powder
4 eggs
2 oz (50g) brown sugar
4 oz (100g) ground almonds
1 tablespoonful orange flower water

Mix the powdered milk with the liquid milk (to make it
more creamy), then heat gently. Beat the eggs together,
with the sugar; pour the heated milk over them and
combine thoroughly. Strain. Stir in the ground almonds
and flower water, and pour into a casserole dish. Stand
this in a baking tray of hot water and bake at
325°F/170°C (Gas Mark 3) for about 40 minutes, or
until set. Eat hot or cold with fruit *purée*, jam, or cream
topping.

Variations
This custard makes an unusual flan. Lightly grease a flan
dish and pack into it a mixture made by combining 2 oz
(50g) melted margarine with 6 oz (175g) digestive
biscuits. Leave to cool, then add filling and cook as
above.

No-Bake Carob Cake

4 oz (100g) margarine
4 oz (100g) brown sugar
1 level tablespoonful carob powder
1 egg
8 oz (225g) digestive biscuits
2 oz (50g) walnuts

Put the margarine and sugar into a saucepan and melt them, stirring all the time. Add the carob powder. Beat the egg lightly, then remove the saucepan from the heat and add the egg to the contents. Mix them quickly and thoroughly. Crush the biscuits into fine crumbs and add them to the other ingredients. Scatter the walnut halves in the bottom of a greased loaf tin, then spoon in the mixture, smoothing the top before placing it in the fridge to firm up.

When ready to serve, turn the cake out of the tin and cut into slices.

Fruit with Nut Cream

1 small melon
2 oz (50g) dates
2 large oranges
¼ pint (150ml) orange juice
1 tablespoonful honey – optional
4 oz (100g) cashew nuts
Water

Chop the melon flesh into cubes; peel and segment the oranges and chop the dates. Divide the fruits between 4 glasses. Mix the orange juice and honey together, and pour a little over each serving of fruit.

In a grinder, make a powder of the cashew nuts, then add sufficient water to make a cream of the consistency you prefer – thick and heavy, or easy to pour. Serve in a jug with the fruit.

Variation
A different kind of 'cream' can be made by whizzing a small carton of cottage cheese in a blender, until smooth. Serve as it is, or topped with a sprinkling of brown sugar. Alternatively, add a tablespoonful of honey to cheese before putting in blender.

Buckwheat Pancakes

8 oz (225g) buckwheat flour
Pinch of salt
1 oz (25g) brown sugar
1 large egg
Approx. 1 pint (575ml) water

Mix the flour and salt together in a bowl. Beat in the egg and sugar, plus enough water to make a batter the consistency of thin cream. Beat well, and leave to stand for 30 minutes. Cook in a heavy pan, and make the pancakes as thin as possible so that they are almost crisp. Serve hot with honey, jam, maple syrup, or a stewed fruit mix such as apples and blackberries.

For a change, add some finely grated orange rind to the mix before cooking, and spread marmalade on the cooked pancake.

Spiced Stewed Rhubarb

2 lb (900g) rhubarb
6 oz (175g) brown sugar
Pinch of cloves
1 teaspoonful cinnamon
Grated rind of 1 orange

Wash the rhubarb and cut into small pieces. Simmer with all the other ingredients, plus enough water to cover fruit, until tender. Drain rhubarb and put into serving dishes. Bring the remaining water quickly to the boil to thicken, then spoon over fruit. Eat hot or cold.

Variation
Make a crumble topping with 4 oz (100g) wholemeal flour, 2 oz (50g) wheat germ, 3 oz (75g) sugar, and 2 oz (50g) margarine. Cook at 350°F/180°C (Gas Mark 4) for about 30 minutes.

Banana-Ginger Flan

6 oz (175g) ginger biscuits
3 oz (75g) margarine
6 large ripe bananas
1 tablespoonful lemon juice
1-2 tablespoonsful honey
¼ pint (150ml) double cream
1 tablespoonful desiccated coconut

Crush biscuits and mix with the melted margarine. Press into a lightly greased flan dish and leave to become firm.

Mash the bananas with the lemon juice and sweeten to taste. Whip the cream until stiff and fold into the banana mixture. Spread over the ginger biscuit base and sprinkle with coconut. Keep in a cool place until required.

Dried Apricot Soufflé

8 oz (225g) dried apricots
4 oz (100g) brown sugar
4 egg whites

Wash and soak the apricots, then press the flesh through a sieve to make a *purée*. Whip the egg whites until stiff, add the sugar. Gently stir all ingredients together, then pour into a greased *soufflé* dish. Bake at 300°F/150°C (Gas Mark 2) for about 45 minutes, and serve at once.

Variations
Using this basic recipe you can make a wide variety of fruit *soufflés*. For example, bananas, prunes, peaches, strawberries, raspberries, pineapple, blackberries and apple − all can be puréed or mashed, and cooked as above.

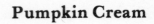

Pumpkin Cream

Approx. ½ lb (225g) pumpkin cut into cubes
Approx. ½ lb (225g) apples, cored, peeled and sliced
2 tablespoonsful oil
Water
2 oz (50g) brown sugar – optional
1 teaspoonful cinnamon
½ teaspoonful ginger
Pinch ground cloves

Heat the oil in a pan, then gently cook the pumpkin and apple, turning frequently, for ten minutes. Add the spices and enough water to just cover the fruit, and cook until soft and creamy. (The natural fruits should be sweet enough, but if you wish to add sugar, do so when you add the water). You may need to mash the *purée* to make it completely smooth. Pour into glasses and leave to cool.

Avocado Whip

4 ripe avocados
3 tablespoonsful lemon juice
5 oz (150g) brown sugar, powdered in grinder
Chopped walnuts or cream

Spoon the avocado flesh out of the skin, mash and then whip it until very light. Stir in the sugar and lemon juice, making sure they are well distributed. Serve in glasses with chopped walnuts, or whipped cream, or both.

Lemon Yogurt Posset

¼ pint (150ml) yogurt
¼ pint (150ml) double cream
2 egg whites
2 tablespoonsful honey
Juice and grated rind of 2 lemons
1 tablespoonful brown sugar, powdered in grinder
1 teaspoonful cinnamon

Put the yogurt and cream into a bowl and whip, then add
the whipped egg whites and combine well. Use a spoon
to stir in the honey, lemon juice, and most of the lemon
rind. Put into glasses and leave to chill. Mix rest of lemon
rind with the sugar and spice, and sprinkle a little onto
the possets when ready to eat them.

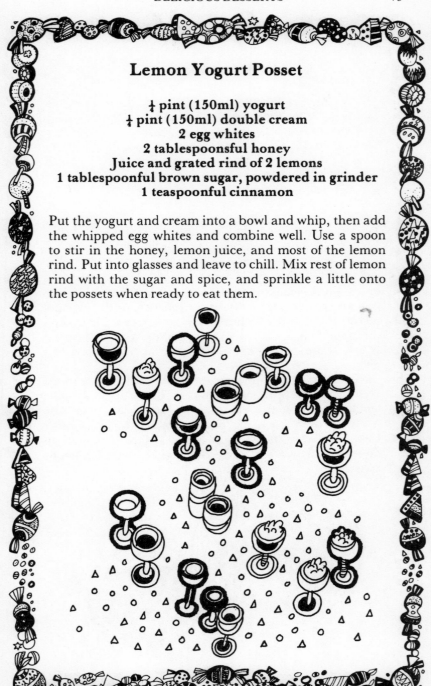

Fruit Flan

For Shortcrust pastry
8 oz (225g) wholemeal flour
4 oz (100g) margarine
2 level teaspoonsful baking powder
Pinch of salt
Approx. 2 tablespoonsful cold water

For filling
1 lb (450g) greengages
2 oz (50g) brown sugar
2 oz (50g) blanched almonds
2 oz (50g) cottage cheese

Combine the flour, baking powder and salt, then use
fingertips to rub in the margarine until mixture
resembles fine breadcrumbs. Add sufficient water to bind
the dough together, and knead lightly. Chill briefly, if
you have time. Roll out carefully to line an 8-inch flan
dish.

Wash, stone and quarter the greengages and arrange
on pastry base. Sprinkle with sugar. Break up or sieve the
cottage cheese so that there are no lumps, and distribute
it evenly over top of the fruit, together with the nuts.
Bake at 400°F/200°C (Gas Mark 6) for about half an
hour, until fruit is soft and pastry light brown. Eat hot or
cold.

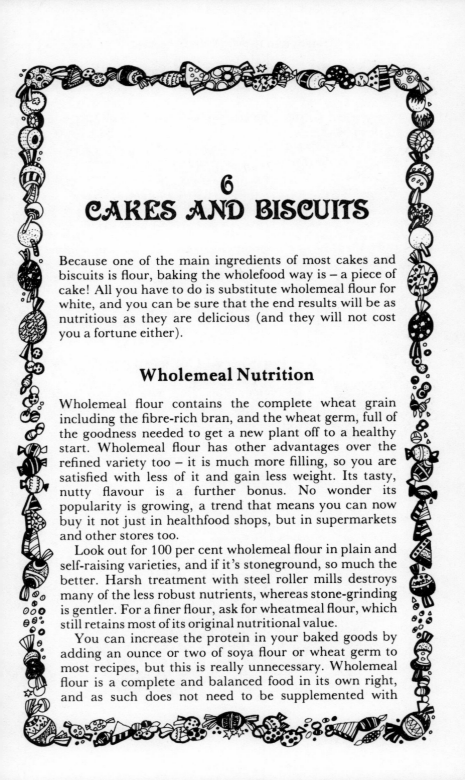

6
CAKES AND BISCUITS

Because one of the main ingredients of most cakes and biscuits is flour, baking the wholefood way is – a piece of cake! All you have to do is substitute wholemeal flour for white, and you can be sure that the end results will be as nutritious as they are delicious (and they will not cost you a fortune either).

Wholemeal Nutrition

Wholemeal flour contains the complete wheat grain including the fibre-rich bran, and the wheat germ, full of the goodness needed to get a new plant off to a healthy start. Wholemeal flour has other advantages over the refined variety too – it is much more filling, so you are satisfied with less of it and gain less weight. Its tasty, nutty flavour is a further bonus. No wonder its popularity is growing, a trend that means you can now buy it not just in healthfood shops, but in supermarkets and other stores too.

Look out for 100 per cent wholemeal flour in plain and self-raising varieties, and if it's stoneground, so much the better. Harsh treatment with steel roller mills destroys many of the less robust nutrients, whereas stone-grinding is gentler. For a finer flour, ask for wheatmeal flour, which still retains most of its original nutritional value.

You can increase the protein in your baked goods by adding an ounce or two of soya flour or wheat germ to most recipes, but this is really unnecessary. Wholemeal flour is a complete and balanced food in its own right, and as such does not need to be supplemented with ingredients other than those you would naturally use when baking.

Use wholemeal flour in any recipe, but if white flour is specified, remember that the bran tends to absorb more moisture, and adjust the liquid content accordingly. Should you have any difficulty handling the dough, leave it in the fridge for half an hour before rolling out, and then do so between sheets of polythene or silver foil. This is particularly useful when forming a large thin layer of dough such as pie topping, as you can pick it up on the supporting sheet, and there is less chance of it breaking.

Always store wholemeal flour in a dry, cool place, and buy it in small quantities so that it does not become stale. Remember, this is a natural food – unlike the refined, processed and preserved flours, it will not stay fresh for ever!

Imaginative Cooking

Although all the recipes that follow are precise in their ingredients and quantities, this does not mean that they will not be equally delicious if adapted to suit what is in your food cupboard. For example, most dried fruits and nuts are interchangeable – and if you like more of one than the other, have more of it! Be imaginative with your use of spices. Experiment with textures by adding rolled oats, toasted wheat germ, chocolate chips (made with brown sugar, of course). Try different sweeteners – molasses, honey, pure maple syrup, all can be used in most cakes and biscuits, and will add their own unique flavour as well as sweetness.

Butterscotch Crunch Bars

2 oz (50g) margarine or butter
8 oz (225g) brown sugar
1 teaspoonful vanilla essence
2 oz (50g) self-raising wholemeal flour
1 egg
3 oz (75g) coarsely chopped walnuts

Grease and line an eight by eight-inch shallow cake tin. Melt the margarine gently over a low heat, add the sugar, and stir until it has dissolved. Pour mixture into a separate bowl and leave to cool a little before adding the vanilla essence. Beat in the egg and, when well combined, stir in the flour. Carefully fold in the walnuts, and pour the mixture into the prepared tin. Make sure that it is spread evenly, and that it fills the corners.

Bake in the centre of the oven at 350°F/180°C (Gas Mark 4) for 25-30 minutes. The cake is cooked when it is firm to touch. Cool in tin, then cut into slices.

Yogurt Banana Bars

4 large ripe bananas
2 eggs
6 oz (175g) honey
1 tablespoonful oil
¼ pint (150ml) natural yogurt
Few drops vanilla essence
8-10 oz (225g-275g) self-raising wholemeal flour
3 teaspoonsful mixed spice
4 oz (100g) sultanas
2 oz (50g) brown sugar

Mash the bananas, then blend well with the eggs. Add the oil and honey and beat together, then stir in the yogurt and vanilla essence, mixing well. In a separate bowl combine the flour and spice, then pour in the banana mix and blend gently but thoroughly. The batter should be thick and smooth – as the sizes of the bananas and eggs can vary, adjust the texture with the amount of flour you add. Distribute the sultanas through the mixture.

Grease a large shallow baking tin, and pour in the batter. Bake at 350°F/180°C (Gas Mark 4) for 30 minutes. Sprinkle the top evenly with sugar just before removing cake from oven – leave a few minutes to dissolve. Cut the cake into handy-sized bars, and leave in the tin until cool.

Carrot Cake

4 oz (100g) margarine
8 oz (225g) brown sugar
4 eggs
4 large carrots, grated fine
4 oz (100g) chopped nuts
1 small apple, chopped fine
8 oz (225g) self-raising wholemeal flour
1 teaspoonful baking powder
2 teaspoonsful cinnamon
$\frac{1}{3}$ pint (200ml) hot water
Pinch of salt

Blend the margarine and sugar, then add the eggs one at a time and beat well. Stir in the carrots, apple and nuts. Sift together the flour, baking powder and cinnamon. Add to mixture gradually, together with the hot water, and combine thoroughly. Add salt. Spoon into a large greased cake tin (or 2 small tins) and bake at 350°F/180°C (Gas Mark 4) for 30-35 minutes.

Date and Apple Slices

**8 oz (225g) wholemeal flour
4 oz (100g) margarine
Approx. 2 tablespoonsful cold water
4 oz (100g) dates
2 medium-sized apples
1 tablespoonful lemon or orange juice
2 oz (50g) hazelnuts
1 oz (25g) desiccated coconut**

Rub margarine into the flour to make a crumb-like mixture, then stir in the water and continue stirring until the flour and margarine stick together. Knead lightly, then wrap the dough in clingfoil or silver foil and chill. Meanwhile, chop the dates and put into a saucepan with the sliced apples and fruit juice. Heat gently, stirring with a wooden spoon until a thick paste is formed. You may need to add extra juice or water if it gets too dry. When ready, roll out the pastry to make two rectangles, and arrange on a greased baking sheet. Use a knife to spread half the fruit mixture on each, then add some chopped hazelnuts and a sprinkling of coconut. Cook in the oven at 425°F/220°C (Gas Mark 7) for about 20 minutes. Cut into slices shortly after taking from the heat, but allow to cool on the baking sheets.

Variations
Chopped peanuts or cashew nuts make a good alternative to the hazelnuts, as do sunflower seeds. Alternatively, spread the pastry with a *purée* of cooked dried apricots and add flaked almonds; or apple and blackberry *purée* with a sprinkling of crunchy granola as a topping. When using fruit *purées*, remove as much liquid as possible or the pastry will go soggy.

Bakewell Tart

6 oz (175g) shortcrust pastry (see page 76)
3 oz (75g) margarine
3 oz (75g) brown sugar
1 large egg
Few drops almond essence
3 oz (75g) ground almonds
1 oz (25g) wholemeal flour
1 oz (25g) wholemeal cake crumbs
2-3 tablespoonsful raspberry jam
1 oz (25g) flaked almonds

Make the pastry and use it to line a seven-inch sandwich
tin. Cream together the margarine and sugar until the
mixture is very fluffy, then gradually beat in the egg and
essence. Combine the flour, crumbs and ground almonds
in a separate bowl, then beat well with the margarine
and sugar. Cover the base of the pastry shell with an even
layer of jam, then spoon the prepared mixture over it and
smooth it with a knife. Top with a sprinkling of flaked
almonds. Bake at 375°F/190°C (Gas Mark 5) for 40
minutes.

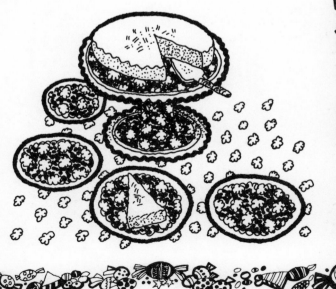

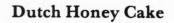

Dutch Honey Cake

12 oz (350g) honey
1 oz (25g) margarine
¼ pint (150ml) milk
8 oz (225g) self-raising wholemeal flour
2 teaspoonsful mixed spice
6 oz (175g) brown sugar
4 oz (100g) candied peel

In a saucepan, gently heat the margarine, honey and milk. When the margarine has completely melted, stir in the sifted flour and spice. Be careful to keep the mixture smooth. Add most of the brown sugar and finally the finely chopped peel. Grease a loaf tin and spoon in the mixture. Bake for 40 minutes at 350°F/180°C (Gas Mark 4), sprinkling the remaining sugar over the cake top shortly before you take it from the oven.

Choux Buns

¼ pint (150ml) water
1 oz (25g) margarine
3 oz (75g) 81 per cent wholemeal flour
2 eggs
¼ pint (150ml) double cream
4 oz (100g) chocolate

Put margarine in a saucepan and add the boiling water. Bring back to boil and, when margarine has melted, stir in the flour. Keep on a low heat and cook gently, still stirring, until the mixture is smooth, thick, and leaves the sides of the pan clean. Take the pan off the heat and allow to cool a little, then beat in one egg at a time, making sure they are thoroughly blended. (If the mixture is too warm the eggs will set.)

Spoon dessertspoonsful of the mixture onto a greased and floured baking tray, and cook in the oven at 400°F/200°C (Gas Mark 6) for about 15 minutes, then reduce to 375°F/190°C (Gas Mark 5) for the last 20 minutes. Buns, when cooked, should look puffed up and should feel firm and crisp to the touch. Leave to cool away from any draughts.

When quite cold, split the buns and fill with the whipped cream. Sandwich them together again. Break chocolate into pieces and place in a bowl over hot water, and stir until completely dissolved. Coat the top of each bun with melted chocolate and leave to set.

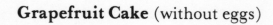

Grapefruit Cake (without eggs)

4 oz (100g) margarine
4 oz (100g) brown sugar
8 oz (225g) self-raising wholemeal flour
4 oz (100g) sultanas
1 teaspoonful mixed spice
¼ pint (150ml) grapefruit juice
2 tablespoonsful finely chopped grapefruit peel

Beat together the margarine and sugar until creamy. In a separate bowl, mix the spices, sultanas and chopped peel into the flour. In a saucepan bring the grapefruit juice to the boil, then remove immediately from the heat. Leave to cool for a few minutes, then pour it into the flour mixture and blend thoroughly. Stir in the margarine and sugar, again making sure that all the ingredients are well mixed together. Spoon into a small, greased loaf tin and flatten the top. Bake at 300°F/150°C (Gas Mark 2) for approximately 1 hour. When cooked, remove from the tin with great care as this is a very crumbly cake. (It is also a very tasty one.)

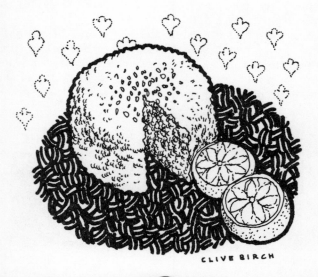

CLIVE BIRCH

Sesame Oat Cookies

6 oz (175g) tahini sesame spread
3 oz (75g) honey
3 oz (75g) sunflower seeds
3 tablespoonsful grated orange peel
6 oz (175g) rolled oats
2-4 tablespoonsful water
1 tablespoonful sesame seeds – optional

Put the tahini and honey together in a bowl and blend well. Stir in the sunflower seeds and orange peel, then add the oats, a spoonful at a time. The mixture should be fairly soft – if it is too dry, add some water to make it the desired consistency.

Drop into small, rough heaps on a greased baking tray, press down lightly, sprinkling a few sesame seeds onto each cookie, if desired. Bake at 375°F/190°C (Gas Mark 5) for approximately 15-20 minutes.

Ginger Biscuits

3 oz (75g) margarine
6 oz (175g) wholemeal flour
3 oz (75g) brown sugar
3 teaspoonsful ground ginger
Pinch of salt
1 large egg yolk

Use fingertips to rub margarine into the flour to make a mixture like fine breadcrumbs. Stir in the sugar, ground ginger and salt. Add the egg yolk to bind the dry ingredients together, and mix well. Roll out as thinly as possible, and use a cup or biscuit cutter to cut discs. Lightly grease a baking sheet and arrange the discs on it – they will not spread much, so you need not leave a lot of space between them. Bake at 375°F/190°C (Gas Mark 5) for about 20 minutes. Allow the biscuits to cool for a while before taking them from the baking sheet.

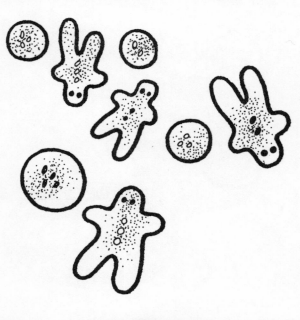

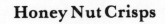

Honey Nut Crisps

2 oz (50g) margarine
2 eggs
4 oz (100g) honey
4 oz (100g) brown sugar
Few drops vanilla essence
4 oz (100g) wholemeal flour
2 oz (50g) hazelnuts

Melt the margarine. Beat the eggs and add them to the margarine, combining well. Add the honey, sugar and essence and stir thoroughly, then fold in the flour. Finally, distribute the finely chopped hazelnuts through the mixture. Grease a baking tray, then drop by spoonfuls onto the tray, leaving space for the biscuits to spread. Cook at 350°F/180°C (Gas Mark 4) for 15-20 minutes. Leave for a while before removing from the tray. The biscuits will crisp up as they cool.

Coconut Macaroons

2 egg whites
5 oz (150g) brown sugar
5 oz (150g) desiccated coconut
Vanilla essence
Pinch of salt
Rice paper

Beat the egg whites lightly until stiff, but not dry. Add the sugar, coconut, a few drops of vanilla essence, and salt. Stir gently until well combined. The mix should have a soft rolling consistency, so if it is too stiff add a few drops of water. If it is too wet, stir in a spoonful of coconut. Put in small heaps on rice paper in a baking tin, leaving room for the macaroons to spread. Bake at 375°F/190°C (Gas Mark 5) for about 20 minutes, until a light golden brown in colour. Allow to cool before you cut or tear the excess rice paper from around each macaroon.

Imperial Biscuits

4 oz (100g) margarine
4 oz (100g) brown sugar
1 egg
8 oz (225g) wholemeal flour
Approx. 4 oz (100g) strawberry jam

Cream together the margarine and sugar until smooth and light. Beat in the egg carefully, then stir in the flour and combine well.

Roll the dough out thinly and cut into small circles. If the dough is difficult to handle, remould and leave in fridge to chill for a while.

Before putting the circles onto a greased baking sheet, use a small cutter (or shaped cardboard) to make a hole in the centre of half of them. Bake for 10-15 minutes at 350°F/180°C (Gas Mark 4).

Use the jam to sandwich together a complete biscuit and one with a hole. Adjust the amount of jam so that, although it shows through the hole it does not ooze out. Leave to set.

Brandy Snaps

4 oz (100g) margarine
4 oz (100g) brown sugar
4 level tablespoonful honey
4 oz (100g) self-raising wholemeal flour
2 level teaspoonsful ground ginger

In a saucepan heat together the margarine, sugar, and honey, stirring well until the margarine melts and the sugar dissolves. Sieve the flour with the ginger, then mix into the slightly cooled margarine. Well grease two baking sheets and drop teaspoonsful of the mixture onto the sheets, allowing room for spreading. Bake for approximately ten minutes at 325°F/170°C (Gas Mark 3) until firm on the edges.

Cool for just two minutes to make handling easier, then remove the snaps one at a time from the baking sheet, and press immediately around the greased handle of a wooden spoon. Hold in place for a few seconds only, then slide off, and put biscuit on a rack to cool completely, and firm up. It is important to work quickly, or the snaps will firm up *before* you have time to roll them. If that happens, a few minutes in a warm oven will soften them again.

Muesli Shortbread

8 oz (225g) margarine
4 oz (100g) brown sugar
8 oz (225g) wholemeal flour
4 oz (100g) muesli
2 oz (50g) raisins (optional)

Beat together the margarine and sugar until soft. Combine the flour and muesli, making sure they are well mixed. Stir the dry ingredients into the margarine and sugar. (If the muesli has only a little dried fruit in it, add some extra raisins for a moist, sweet contrast to the drier crunchy biscuit). Grease a Swiss roll tin. Press the mixture into it and bake at 300°F/150°C (Gas Mark 2) for 30 minutes. Cut into slices shortly after the shortbread comes out of the oven, but do not remove from the tin until cold.

Brazil Nutties

4 oz (100g) margarine
4 oz (100g) brown sugar
1 egg
4 oz (100g) ground brazil nuts
6 oz (175g) wholemeal flour
10 brazil nuts

Put the margarine into a bowl with the sugar and cream together well. Add the beaten egg. In another bowl combine the flour and ground nuts, then put together the contents of the two bowls and mix thoroughly.

Grease a baking tray and drop spoonsful of the mixture onto it. Press each biscuit lightly, and scatter some roughly chopped brazil nuts on the top. Bake at 350°F/180°C (Gas Mark 4) for 15 minutes, or until firm to touch.

7
PARTY-TIME FAVOURITES

Just the mention of childhood parties conjures up, for most people, the tastes, smells and colours of all those traditional party-time favourites – jellies and jam tarts, trifles and toffee apples, and of course a mouth-watering cake complete with icing sugar and candles. The gifts may have been welcome, the games great fun, but the food was most often the real highlight of the afternoon's festivities.

Today's children may be a little more sophisticated, and are most probably better fed, but they still think that parties are very special occasions. So, it would not be fair to let them down by dishing up the foods they eat all week.

This does not mean you have to change your whole attitude to food, or even use different ingredients. Once you have decided that wholefoods make sense, it would be nonsense to put aside that decision on special occasions. It would also be positively harmful – you would be teaching your children, by implication, that wholefoods are not good enough to grace the table at party-time. From such seeds can grow a reverence for refined foods, with their bright colours and strong flavours, and a growing child can be very determined about what he will and will not eat.

Party Preparation

What you may have to do, instead, is spend some extra time in the kitchen. One of the first rules for a successful party is to set the table with an array of different items. Children often enjoy the look of the food as much as the taste, especially if it's colourful and attractively arranged, and they get a lot of pleasure too from being able to choose for themselves. So instead of making a huge batch of one kind of cake or biscuit, make two or three different varieties, cut them into assorted shapes and decorate and flavour them in various ways. (You can, of course, let your own children help you in the kitchen – they will probably enjoy that as much as the party). Many of the recipes given here are actually much quicker and simpler than you may think.

Cooking a special dish whilst the party is in progress can go down well for entertainment value, but it does mean preparing as much as possible beforehand, and having someone around to keep an eye on the children whilst you do your bit. Fruit fritters are quite simple, and popcorn is even easier. Pancakes are very popular, but you would probably be wise to cook them in advance, and just hot them up when needed.

The recipes given here use wholefoods as far as possible – they may taste slightly different from the shop-bought varieties, but they should still go down a treat with your party visitors. Try other recipes substituting brown flour and sugar for the refined varieties, and eliminate empty decorations, using instead nuts and dried fruits.

Toffee Apples

4 oz (100g) butter or margarine
1 lb (450g) brown sugar
2 tablespoonsful water
8 small eating apples

Combine the butter, sugar and water, and heat gently, stirring with a wooden spoon until the sugar has completely dissolved. Bring mixture slowly to the boil, then continue cooking until toffee reaches 280°F/137°C (soft crack stage). Wipe the apples to ensure they are clean – shiny skins should be roughened a little with a fine grater, or the toffee may not stick very well. Remove stalks from apples, then insert a stick into the stalk end as firmly as possible. Dip the apples one at a time into the toffee mixture, tipping the pan if necessary to coat each apple completely and evenly. Then dip briefly into a bowl of very cold water. Stand apples on waxed paper or a rack, and leave to dry.

These toffee apples do not keep very well, so make them no earlier than the day before the party.

Banana Tarts

8 oz (225g) 81 per cent wholemeal flour*
2 level teaspoonsful baking powder
4 oz (100g) margarine
Approx. 2 tablespoonsful water
4 large firm but ripe bananas
3 tablespoonsful apricot jam
2 tablespoonsful water

Sift together the flour and baking powder, then use fingertips to rub the margarine into the flour to make a breadcrumb-like mixture. Pour in the 2 tablespoonsful of cold water and, using a fork, mix until the dough binds. Chill briefly before rolling out between 2 sheets of greaseproof paper. Use a cup or biscuit cutter to divide the dough into about twelve small discs, then arrange in greased tart tins. Prick lightly with a fork and bake blind at 375°F/190°C (Gas Mark 5) for about ten minutes. Remove from oven, cool, then remove from tins.

Heat together the jam and water to make a syrup. Slice the bananas and share them equally between the tarts. Brush the cooled syrup over the bananas to give a glaze finish, making sure you cover them completely. Alternatively, gently mix the banana slices into the syrup before dividing between the tart cases.

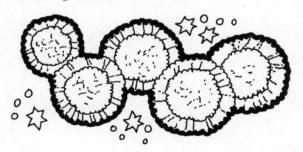

*You can use 100 per cent wholemeal flour, of course, but it is a little difficult to handle. As individual tarts are more fiddly than most pastry recipes, you can make your task easier by using the finer flour.

Gingerbread Men

4 oz (100g) margarine
6 oz (175g) honey
¼ pint (150ml) water
Approx. 8 oz (225g) wholemeal flour
2 teaspoonsful ground ginger
1 teaspoonful mixed spice
Pinch of Salt
Nuts and raisins for decoration (optional)

Melt the margarine gently in a saucepan, then add the honey and water and stir well. Sift together the flour and spices. Stir into the syrup gradually, using enough to make the dough a stiff but pliable consistency. Roll up in clingfoil or silver foil, and put into the fridge for at least half an hour so that rolling it out is easier.

Roll to a thickness of approx. half an inch and use a man-shaped biscuit cutter to divide the dough. Gingerbread men hardly need decorating, but if you wish to make yours more special, use nuts and raisins to make eyes, a mouth, and buttons down the front. Place onto a greased baking sheet and cook in the oven at 350°F/180°C (Gas Mark 4) for about 15 minutes. Leave to cool for a while before removing them from the sheet.

Coconut Pyramids

8 oz (225g) desiccated coconut
4 oz (100g) brown sugar
2 eggs
Rice paper
Glacé **cherries (optional)**

Mix the coconut with the sugar, then blend in the beaten eggs. Continue stirring until the mixture is a soft dropping consistency. Press spoonsful of the coconut mixture into an eggcup to get the familiar 'pyramid' shape, then turn out onto a sheet of rice paper placed in a tin. (If no rice paper is available, either put the pyramids onto buttered greaseproof paper, or straight onto the tin, making sure it is well greased and floured first).

A *glacé* cherry should be pressed firmly onto each pyramid at this stage. Bake at 350°F/180°C (Gas Mark 4) for 15 minutes. Cool for a short while before cutting the excess rice paper from around the pyramid.

Because of the coarser sugar (white castor sugar is traditional in this recipe) your pyramids will be more golden than usual, and deliciously crunchy.

Popcorn

**4 oz (100g) popping corn
2 oz (50g) brown sugar (or more, as needed)
2 tablespoonsful oil (or more, as needed)**

Heat the oil over a high flame in a saucepan that has a well-fitting lid. Sprinkle in the sugar, then a generous handful of popcorn, and cover. Continue cooking until the corn starts to pop, then – still on the heat – shake the saucepan so that the contents are well mixed. The popcorn is ready when the noisy activity comes to a halt! Tip it into a dish and cook another handful, adding sugar and oil if necessary.

Variations

Omit the sugar, and pour a thin sweet sauce (made with jam or honey and a little water) over the cooked popcorn, stirring it in lightly.

Omit the sugar and sprinkle the cooked popcorn with a little soya sauce, for children with more savoury tastes.

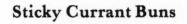

Sticky Currant Buns

1 lemon
8 oz (225g) self-raising wholemeal flour
Pinch salt
6 oz (175g) margarine
6 oz (175g) brown sugar
3 eggs
4 oz (100g) currants
2 tablespoonsful honey
Pinch mixed spice

Remove peel from lemon, and grate enough to fill a tablespoon. Set aside rest of lemon. Sift flour and salt into a mixing bowl; add margarine, sugar, eggs, grated lemon peel and currants. Stir well together – if mixture is very stiff you may need to add a spoonful of warm water.

Grease about 20 patty tins, then fill two-thirds full with prepared mixture. Bake at 425°F/220°C (Gas Mark 7) for 15 minutes. Whilst buns are cooking, prepare a glaze topping by gently heating the chopped lemon flesh with the honey and spice. Stir occasionally. Take buns from oven and, using a brush, glaze the top of each with the honey sauce. Cook five minutes longer.

Trifle

4 wholemeal sponge cakes
8 oz (225g) fresh raspberries
2 oz (50g) brown sugar
1 packet agar agar raspberry jelly
½ pint whipping cream

For custard
½ pint (275ml) milk
1 egg
1 egg yolk
1 oz (25g) brown sugar

For decoration
2 oz (50g) flaked almonds, lightly toasted
2 oz (50g) desiccated coconut

Wash the raspberries, then cook with the sugar and a little water until softened but not mushy. Split the sponge cakes and arrange across the bottom of a bowl; top with most of the cooked raspberries and juice.

Make up the jelly according to instructions, but use about ¼ pint (150ml) less water than usual. Pour jelly into bowl and leave to set.

To make the custard, warm the milk without letting it boil. Whisk the egg and egg yolk, add the sugar, then pour onto the milk and whisk together. Continue cooking gently, stirring to keep the custard smooth, until it thickens. Remove from heat and set aside to cool slightly before pouring it over the set jelly. Leave until cold. Whip the cream until thick. Spread over the custard, and sprinkle with coconut, then arrange the flaked almonds and remaining raspberries in an attractive pattern.

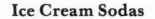

Ice Cream Sodas

1 pint (575ml) milk
1 pint (575ml) soda water
6 oz (175g) blackberries
2 oz (50g) honey
A little water
4 scoops ice cream

Clean the fruit, then simmer it for just a few minutes with the honey and enough water to stop it sticking. Leave the fruit *purée* to cool. Divide it equally between four tall soda glasses, add a scoop of ice cream, then top up with the milk and soda water. Serve at once.

You can use any fruit for this recipe and any flavour of ice cream. Mashed bananas (which need no cooking) taste delicious with a nutty ice cream. Apple is good with a scoop of chocolate ice cream, and strawberries with honey yogurt ice cream.

Jam Roll

2 eggs
2 oz (50g) brown sugar
2 oz (50g) self-raising wholemeal flour (81 per cent
or 100 per cent)
1 tablespoonful hot water
3 tablespoonsful jam of your choice
1 oz (25g) brown sugar, powdered in grinder

Line a Swiss roll tin with greased greaseproof paper. Separate eggs, and whisk the whites until just becoming stiff, then whisk in the yolks and sugar. Use a metal spoon to fold the sieved flour into the egg mixture, and finally stir in the hot water.

Spread the mixture in the prepared tin, making sure it is even, and bake in a pre-heated oven at 425°F/220°C (Gas Mark 7) for seven or eight minutes. It is important to remove the sponge from the heat the moment it is ready, i.e. when you can press it gently with your finger and leave no impression. Over-cooking will make it difficult to roll.

Leave to cool, then remove from the greaseproof paper and spread with warmed jam. Make a shallow cut in the roll about 1 inch (2.5 cm) from the end nearest to you, which makes it easier to roll. Continue rolling firmly and neatly. Sprinkle with powdered brown sugar. Serve just as it is, cut into slices. Alternatively, make it into something even more special by topping each slice with a scoop of vanilla ice cream or whipped cream, to be eaten with a spoon.

Apple Fritters

4 oz (100g) self-raising wholemeal flour
2 eggs
¼ pint (150ml) milk (or milk and water)
Pinch of salt
4 medium-sized cooking apples
1 oz (25g) wholemeal flour
2 oz (50g) brown sugar
Oil for frying

Sieve together the self-raising flour and salt, add the milk and then the egg yolks. Mix well until the batter is thick and smooth. Beat the egg whites until stiff, and fold gently into batter.

Peel and core the apples carefully, then cut into thin slices. Dust with the extra flour so that the batter sticks as you dip each apple slice into it. Fry the fritters (preferably in deep oil, although shallow frying can be used) until crisp and golden. It is important to cook them on a medium heat – fritters cooked too quickly will be over-cooked on the outside, raw and lukewarm on the inside.

Remove from pan, drain on absorbent paper, and sprinkle with sugar. Serve on plate, or – the way most children prefer – in paper napkin envelopes.

Variations
Most fruits can be used to make fritters. Halved bananas, pineapple rings and small pears are particularly popular.

Shredded Wheat Treats

4 Shredded Wheat biscuits
4 tablespoonsful honey
4 tablespoonsful water
4 small bananas
Vanilla ice cream
Granola or other crunchy cereal (see pp 44, 45)

Combine the honey and water, heat gently, then add the Shredded Wheat biscuits and continue cooking until they become soft, but still retain their shapes. Spoon each one onto a plate, pour on remaining liquid. Cut the bananas in half, lengthwise, and place on top of biscuits, add a good dollop of ice cream and a sprinkling of a crunchy cereal such as Granola. Chopped or flaked roasted nuts are also good as a contrast to the smooth cool texture of the ice cream, and the sweetness of the banana. Alternatively, try toasted wheat germ. Another variation is to use real cream instead of ice cream.

Meringues

**2 egg whites
4 oz (100g) brown sugar**

Whisk the egg whites until so stiff they remain in place when the bowl is turned upside down. Carefully fold in the sugar, a spoonful at a time, until well distributed. Put the mixture in small, neat spoonfuls onto a greased baking tray, and bake in a very slow oven at 225°F/110°C (Gas Mark ¼) for 1½-3 hours, depending on the size. Meringues should be cooked on the outside, but soft inside – test by pressing the undersides gently with your thumb. Makes about 20 small meringues.

Variations
Add a teaspoonful very finely grated lemon or orange rind; some finely chopped walnuts; or an ounce or two of wholewheat flakes.

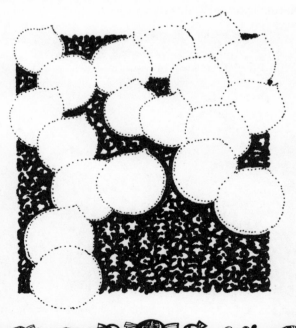

Peanut Butter Cookies

4 oz (100g) smooth or crunchy peanut butter
4 oz (100g) margarine
2 oz (50g) brown sugar
2 eggs
4 oz (100g) self-raising wholemeal flour
1 teaspoonful cinnamon
Pinch of salt
2 oz (50g) raisins

Combine the margarine, sugar and peanut butter, beating well until smooth, then add the eggs. Beat again. Sift the flour with the salt and spice, then fold into the peanut butter mixture. Add the raisins, stirring thoroughly so that all ingredients are blended, and the dried fruit evenly distributed. Use a spoon to drop small mounds of the mixture onto a baking tray, leaving space between them for spreading. Bake at 350°F/180°C (Gas Mark 4) for 10-15 minutes, or until gold in colour and firm to touch.

This recipe makes about 40 cookies. If that is too many for your needs, either halve the ingredients given, or make the full batch and keep some of them for eating later – providing they are stored in an airtight container they stay fresh for ages.

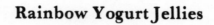

Rainbow Yogurt Jellies

1 packet agar agar strawberry or raspberry jelly
1 packet agar agar greengage jelly
1 packet agar agar lemon jelly
1½ pints (850ml) natural yogurt

Make up the three jellies in the normal way, each in its own bowl, and put aside to chill. Just before they start to set, fold half a pint of yogurt into each jelly and chill again, but do not let it set. Whisk the jellies until light and frothy. Using tall sundae glasses, put a portion of the red jelly at the bottom of each, top with a portion of the green, and finish with some yellow jelly. Stand the glasses in a cool place until jellies are completely set.

Makes approximately 16 helpings.

If you have time to spare, this recipe would obviously be more nutritious still if made with 3 different kinds of fresh fruit juice (for example, apple, redcurrant and lemon) and agar agar. For guidance, you need about 2 level teaspoonsful agar agar to set 1 pint (550ml) of liquid.

Molasses Flapjacks

**4 oz (100g) margarine
1 oz (25g) molasses
3 oz (75g) brown sugar
6 oz (175g) rolled oats
2 oz (50g) wheat germ
Pinch of salt**

Grease an eleven-inch by seven-inch shallow cake or Swiss roll tin. Melt the margarine in a small saucepan, together with the molasses and sugar. In a separate bowl, combine the oats and wheat germ, then add them to the molasses syrup with the salt, and stir until thoroughly mixed.

Spread the mixture over the prepared tin, using a knife to ensure it goes out to the edges, is even, and smooth on top.

Bake in the centre of the oven at 400°F/200°C (Gas Mark 6) for about 15 minutes, until firm to touch. Leave to cool slightly, then cut into fingers, but do not attempt to remove from the tin until quite cold.

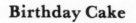

Birthday Cake

For cake
6 oz (175g) margarine
6 oz (175g) brown sugar
3 large eggs
6 oz (175g) self-raising wholemeal flour
1 lb (450g) tin pineapple pieces in natural juice

For icing and decoration
4 oz (100g) butter (preferably unsalted)
4-6oz (100-175g) brown sugar, powdered in grinder
1 orange
1-2 tablespoonsful orange juice
2 oz (50g) whole blanched almonds

Grease and line two seven-inch sandwich tins. In a mixing bowl, cream the margarine with the sugar until light and fluffy. Beat eggs and add to mix, combining them well. Stir in a little of the sieved flour, together with 2 tablespoonsful of the pineapple juice and half the pineapple chopped fine. Now fold in the rest of the flour and the bran left in the sieve. Spoon the mixture into the two prepared tins, smooth the tops, and bake at 375°F/190°C (Gas Mark 5) for 25-30 minutes. Cool before decorating.

Cream together the butter and ground brown sugar – the amount of sugar used will enable you to vary the texture of the butter icing to suit your own requirements. Peel the orange, keeping the fruit itself intact. Finely grate some of the peel, and add about 3 tablespoonsful of it to the icing, along with the extra orange juice. Blend well. Use half the mixture to sandwich together the two cake rounds and spread the rest of it over the top of the cake. Use the almonds and remainder of the pineapple to make a design on top of the cake, and the segmented orange to form a 'flower' for the centre. (Optional – brush fruit with some juice in which a little sugar has been dissolved for a shiny surface).

8
JAMS AND
SWEET SPREADS

There is nothing quite like the taste of homemade jams.
Country folk have long been preserving autumn fruits for
winter eating in this delicious way, and it is a process
that is well worth learning.

The added advantage for the wholefooder is that you
make your jam as pure and wholesome as jams used to
be. Your family will be able to enjoy jam without eating
the mass-produced, brightly coloured shop-bought
variety, manufactured out of white sugar, preservatives,
flavouring, and other such wonders of science. Your
jams will be made from fresh-picked fruits, raw brown
sugar or honey. They will have lots of flavour, so you will
only need to use them in small amounts. And you will be
able to ring the changes, experiment with different
ingredients, maybe come up with a recipe or two that are
quite unlike anything else, so that simple bread and jam
become a real treat – just like it used to be.

Jam can, of course, be eaten in a variety of other ways.
It can be used to top or fill cakes, as a sauce for ice cream,
a flavouring for plain yogurt. Put it in pancakes, tarts,
muesli, rice puddings. Eat with cream cheese, cottage
cheese, curd cheese. Stir a little into whipped cream to
give it colour and sweetness. Use it to glaze fresh fruits.
Some jams can be eaten as a dessert – just put into a
bowl and add a spoonful of single cream and a sprinkling
of nuts.

Basic Rules

Here, then, are some basic rules for jam-making. Start by

picking firm, ripe fruit, preferably in season. To cook it, use a large thick pan so there is room for the jam to boil without boiling over! Always cook the fruit slowly to soften the skins, extract the natural pectin (setting substance) and to ensure the jam is an attractive colour. Make sure the sugar is completely dissolved before boiling the jam (otherwise it may burn or crystallize) then boil rapidly without stirring.

The time a jam takes to reach setting point may vary from 3 to 5 minutes, and as many jams will not set if boiled too long, it is important to start testing early. To do this, chill a saucer (preferably in a refrigerator) then drop a little jam onto it and leave to cool. If, when touched, the jam wrinkles, it is set.

Any jam that contains no whole fruit should be poured immediately into hot, dry, clean jars. Jam containing fruit pieces should be left to stiffen a little, then stirred so that fruit is evenly distributed. Fill the jars right to the top – less air space means less chance of the jam becoming mouldy. Cover at once with waxed discs, wax side down, then add cellophane cover and seal with an elastic band or sealing tape. Store in a cool, dark, dry cupboard.

A variety of spreads can be made much more quickly and easily, using fruits or other ingredients, and can be eaten in the same ways as jam. However, they will not keep for anywhere near as long, and should be stored in a refrigerator.

On the following pages you will find a number of recipes to try, but they are just to get you started. More specialized books will give you countless alternatives to try; you could also build up on the methods given here, and create some of your own. If you follow the basic rules, you cannot go far wrong.

Rose Hip Jam

**1 lb (450g) rose hips
1 lb (450g) apples
12 oz (350g) brown sugar
1¼ pints (850ml) water**

Wash the rose hips, then scoop out the seeds, and simmer the hips in the water for about two hours. Cool. Strain the juice through muslin and add to it the peeled, cored and sliced apples and sugar. Bring quickly to the boil, then lower heat and boil gently until setting point is reached. Pour into hot, dry, sterilized jars at once. Fill to top and seal.

Apple Ginger Jelly

**2 lb (900g) cooking apples
1 pint (575ml) water
Brown sugar
2 teaspoonsful ground ginger**

Chop the apples into smallish pieces, but do not peel or core. Simmer in the water until the fruit turns to a pulp. Put the pulp into muslin and leave to strain, preferably overnight. Measure the juice in a jug, and allow 1 lb (450g) of sugar to each pint (575ml) of liquid. Put the juice, sugar and ginger into a saucepan and bring to boil, then continue boiling rapidly until setting point is reached. Pour into jars at once and seal tightly.

Carrot Jam

1 lb (450g) carrot pulp
1 lb (450g) brown sugar
Grated rind of 1 medium lemon
Juice of 2 lemons

You will probably need about 4 lbs (1.8kg) of carrots to make 1 lb (450g) pulp. Do this by washing and peeling the carrots, then cut into pieces and cook in water. When soft enough, press through a sieve and weigh the pulp. (If it comes to more, simply adjust the other ingredients accordingly; for example, with 1½ lb (675g) pulp you will need 1½ lb (675g) sugar, rind of 1 large lemon and juice of 3 lemons.)

Boil the pulp with the other ingredients gently until setting point is reached. Put into clean jars and seal.

Banana Jam

2 lb (900g) bananas
2½ pints (1.5 litres) pineapple juice
2 lemons
1½ lb (675g) brown sugar
½ pint (275ml) water

Put the chopped bananas into a saucepan with the pineapple juice, water, sugar and juice from the freshly squeezed lemons. Heat to boiling point, then turn down heat and cook ingredients, stirring frequently for approximately 30 minutes. Jam is ready to be turned into clean warmed jars when it is thick and smooth.

Rhubarb Jam

2 lb (900g) fresh rhubarb
2 lb (900g) brown sugar
8 oz (225g) dried figs
Juice of one lemon
Juice of one orange

Wash the figs and pat dry, then cut into very small pieces. Do the same with the rhubarb. Combine all the ingredients and leave overnight. Put them into a pan and bring to the boil, then continue boiling rapidly until the jam reaches setting point. Allow to cool in the pan until it stiffens slightly, stir to distribute fruit evenly, and pour into jars. Seal tightly.

CLIVE BIRCH

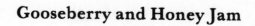

Gooseberry and Honey Jam

1 lb (450g) gooseberries
8 oz (225g) brown sugar
8 oz (225g) honey
¼-½ pint (150-275ml) water

Top and tail the washed gooseberries, and cook gently in sufficient water to just cover fruit. As cooking time will vary depending on whether fruit is ripe or more firm, adjust the water accordingly. Simmer until soft enough to make into a pulp.

Add the honey and sugar and bring rapidly to boil, stirring to make sure sugar dissolves completely. Continue boiling, stirring occasionally to prevent sticking. After five minutes start to check if jam has reached setting point – when you use honey in a jam, crystals may start to form if you boil the mixture for too long. When ready, put jam immediately into hot jars and seal.

Honey can be used in this proportion in most jam recipes, and will give a smoothness and flavour that is quite unique. It may change the texture of the jam slightly.

Three-Fruit Marmalade

2 grapefruits
4 lemons   } together these should weigh
2 sweet oranges   3 lb (1.4kg)

6 lb (2.7kg) brown sugar
6 pints (3.4 litres) water

Wash and halve the fruit, squeeze out the juice and set aside. Remove the peel carefully and cut, shred or mince it. Place the peel and the water in a bowl, and add the discarded white pith and pips which should be tied firmly in a piece of muslin. (They add flavour, but must be removed before adding the sugar). Soak overnight.

Simmer the mixture gently for about an hour until the peel is tender. Remove muslin bag and squeeze any juice trapped in it back into the saucepan. Add the sugar and the juice from the fruit, and stir until sugar dissolves, then boil the marmalade rapidly, without stirring again, until setting point is reached. Test early, and continue testing frequently. The setting period is quite short and it is important to remove the marmalade from the heat the moment it reaches that point, or it will never set properly.

Allow marmalade to cool a little, then stir before pouring into hot sterilized jars.

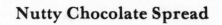

Nutty Chocolate Spread

**8 oz (225g) plain chocolate
4 oz (100g) roasted hazelnuts
1-2 tablespoonsful oil
2 tablespoonsful skimmed-milk powder
1-2 oz (25-50g) sugar, powdered in grinder.**

Grind the nuts. Melt the chocolate in a bowl over hot water, and stir in the ground hazelnuts, mixing well. Add the milk powder, and enough oil to make the mixture smooth and creamy. This spread has a unique flavour, and should not be too sweet – however, if you find it too sharp, stir in some sugar to taste.

Keep in a screwtop jar somewhere cool.

Lemon Curd

3 large lemons
8 oz (225g) brown sugar
4 oz (100g) margarine
2 eggs

Remove the rind from all three lemons and grate it as finely as possible. Squeeze the juice from two lemons. Put the margarine, sugar, lemon rind and juice into a double saucepan or bowl placed over a pan of hot water. Use a wooden spoon to stir from time to time, until the sugar has dissolved and the margarine melted. Whisk the eggs lightly in a separate bowl, and add them slowly to the mixture, still keeping it over the heat, and stirring constantly. Continue doing so until the mixture becomes thick and creamy smooth, which will take about 15 minutes. If any of the egg white should coagulate, just remove it with a spoon.

Pour into warmed jars and seal. Will keep approximately 1 month.

Variation
Orange curd can be made in exactly the same way, but instead of the lemon, use the rind of three oranges, and juice of two. For grapefruit curd, use rind of one grapefruit and juice of two.

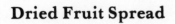

Dried Fruit Spread

**6 oz (175g) sultanas
6 oz (175g) dried apricots
6 oz (175g) honey
Juice and rind of a lemon**

Soak the dried fruit, preferably overnight, then simmer until very soft. Drain, then put all the ingredients into a blender and make into a *purée*. If you do not have a blender, rub the soaked fruit through a sieve to break it up, then mix with other ingredients. The result should be a thick, smooth spread – add a little of the water in which the fruit was cooked if the spread is too stiff. Put into sterilized jars and keep in fridge.

Blackberry and Apple Spread

**3 lb (1.4kg) blackberries
1 lb (450g) apples
Approx. 3 tablespoonsful honey**

Wash the blackberries and put into a heavy saucepan with the cored, chopped apples, and enough water to barely cover the fruit. Bring to the boil, then simmer gently for an hour, stirring frequently to prevent burning. Sweeten with honey to taste, then cook gently approximately half an hour more, still stirring occasionally.

Pour into sterilized jars and seal tightly.

Honey Nut Spread

2 oz (50g) margarine
2 oz (50g) finely chopped brazil nuts
3 tablespoonsful honey
2 teaspoonsful cinnamon – optional

Blend all ingredients together well. Keep in covered jar in fridge.

Sweet Cottage Cheese Spread

Small carton cottage cheese
1 tablespoonful finely grated lemon rind
1 tablespoonful honey

Drain any excess liquid from the cottage cheese, then mix all ingredients together well, and put in a jar in the fridge. The flavours blend especially well if left overnight. Eat the spread within three or four days.

Strawberry Spread

8 oz (225g) ripe strawberries
1 tablespoonful honey
1 tablespoonful orange juice

Mash the fruit to a soft *purée*. Add the other ingredients and mix in thoroughly. Put into a sterilized jar, and keep in the fridge.

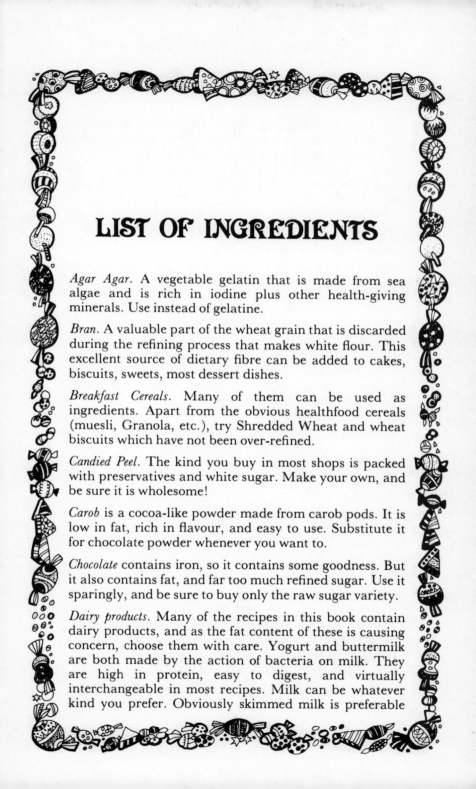

LIST OF INGREDIENTS

Agar Agar. A vegetable gelatin that is made from sea algae and is rich in iodine plus other health-giving minerals. Use instead of gelatine.

Bran. A valuable part of the wheat grain that is discarded during the refining process that makes white flour. This excellent source of dietary fibre can be added to cakes, biscuits, sweets, most dessert dishes.

Breakfast Cereals. Many of them can be used as ingredients. Apart from the obvious healthfood cereals (muesli, Granola, etc.), try Shredded Wheat and wheat biscuits which have not been over-refined.

Candied Peel. The kind you buy in most shops is packed with preservatives and white sugar. Make your own, and be sure it is wholesome!

Carob is a cocoa-like powder made from carob pods. It is low in fat, rich in flavour, and easy to use. Substitute it for chocolate powder whenever you want to.

Chocolate contains iron, so it contains some goodness. But it also contains fat, and far too much refined sugar. Use it sparingly, and be sure to buy only the raw sugar variety.

Dairy products. Many of the recipes in this book contain dairy products, and as the fat content of these is causing concern, choose them with care. Yogurt and buttermilk are both made by the action of bacteria on milk. They are high in protein, easy to digest, and virtually interchangeable in most recipes. Milk can be whatever kind you prefer. Obviously skimmed milk is preferable for anyone concerned about fat and/or cholesterol intake, and it can be made to give creamier-tasting results by adding extra skimmed milk powder. Keep double cream for very special occasions, or use it in a mix with yogurt or single cream. Butter too should be kept to a minimum. Its fat content can be lowered by substituting some of it with a low cholesterol soft margarine.

Dried fruits. The original healthfood 'sweet', as they contain a very high percentage of natural sugar, minerals and vitamins. Dates are particularly rich in niacin, figs are rich in iron and apricots in vitamin A. (Slimmers might like to know that prunes are the least fattening.) When buying dried fruit, you should choose the untreated variety.

Essences/extracts. Unfortunately, there does not seem to be a range on the market that is natural; all such flavourings appear to be the result of a manufacturing process. The very best way to flavour your cooking is obviously by using the real thing – raspberry juice for raspberry flavouring (and colour), etc. As this is not always possible, I suggest you use the alternatives with care, and as infrequently as possible.

Flour. When baking use 100 per cent wholemeal flour as often as possible. For lighter results, you can also cook with 81 per cent wholemeal flour, which has had 19 per cent of the coarser particles removed. Add more protein to sweets, cakes and desserts by sprinkling in some soya flour, which is made from soya beans.

Fruit Juices. Use fresh whenever possible; frozen as an alternative. Only use tinned fruit juices when you have no other choice. They have little goodness left in them, but can be useful when you want something more exotic than usual, such as pineapple juice.

Honey. One of the most natural, easily digested forms of sweetening. Its subtle tastes can be swamped if other ingredients are too strong, so as it is an expensive item, use it with care. Buy pure, untreated varieties if possible.

Jams/Marmalades. Whenever these are mentioned in the recipes, try to use one made with raw sugar only. Better still, make them yourself.

Molasses. A rich, concentrated, highly distinctive syrup that contains iron, copper, calcium, magnesium, and much more. As it is strongly flavoured, start by using it sparingly – but DO use it, it is a valuable food. Some molasses are treated with sulphur dioxide, so try to find a variety that has not been processed.

Nuts/seeds. Buy them raw, in small quantities, and add them to your cooking with confidence. All nuts and seeds provide protein, texture, taste, and are amazingly adaptable.

Oil. Always use vegetable oils such as sunflower, safflower, soya, corn. Cold-pressed oils are preferable.

Plantmilk. This can be used in most of the recipes without affecting the results.

Rolled Oats. They have valuable amino acids, which may explain how so many ancient Britons survived on oats as a staple food for so long! They add bulk and crunch to baking as well as nourishment.

Sugar. Refined white sugar is now being blamed for a multitude of illnesses and problems. Raw brown sugar is preferable as it does offer small amounts of minerals and some B-vitamins, but should still be kept to a minimum in a wholefood diet. Be careful, too, that you are buying *raw* brown sugar, and not refined sugar that has been dyed.

Tahini is a sort of butter made from sesame seeds. It has a strong, distinctive taste that makes it an ideal savoury food – but it is also surprisingly good with sweet ingredients, especially honey. As sesame seeds are a very good source of protein, tahini is a valuable food. Use it often.

Tofu. Another protein-rich ingredient to incorporate into your sweet cookery. It is made from soya beans, and has a bland taste that means you can flavour it in whatever way you wish.

Vinegar. Cider vinegar, especially that made from organically grown apples, is to be chosen in preference to any other kind. Its taste can be stronger than malt vinegar, so be sparing when you first use it.

Wheat germ. This is the embryo of the wheat, the life force. It contains protein, vitamins, minerals, and is good for everything from losing weight to gaining weight, from falling hair to fatigue. Add it to whatever you are cooking in small amounts, or eat it with stewed fruit, cereals, milk and honey. It is available raw and toasted, and sometimes with sweetening added.

Yogurt. Also called 'The Milk of Eternal Life'. Low in fat and calories, rich in protein, it is very adaptable and not used nearly as often in cookery as it could be. Try it in baking, as a substitute for cream with desserts, on its own or flavoured with raw sugar jams as well as with the more traditional fruit *purée*.

INDEX